Sic Evenit Ratio

ut Componitur

Sic Evenit Ratio ut Componitur

The small book about large system change

Dr. Sir John Oldham

Kingsham

First published in 2004
by Kingsham Press

Oldbury Complex
Marsh Lane
Easthampnett
Chichester, West Sussex
PO18 0JW
United Kingdom

© 2004, John Oldham

Typeset in Palatino Light
by Marie Doherty

Printed and bound by
St. Richard's Press
Terminus Road
Chichester
West Sussex
UK

ISBN: 1-904235-27-1

All rights reserved. No part of this book may be reprinted or reproduced or utilised in any form or by any electronic, mechanical, or other means, now known or later invented, including photocopying and recording, or in any information storage or retrieval system, without the prior permission in writing from the publishers.

British Library Cataloguing in Publication Data
A catalogue record of this book is available from the British Library

Oldham, John

Contents

About the author   vii
Preface   xi
Foreword   xiii

Chapter 1: Background   1

Chapter 2: Sic evenit ratio ut componitur   11

Chapter 3: Systematic transfer of knowledge   17

Chapter 4: Creating an environment that facilitates the uptake of ideas   25

Chapter 5: Strategy, policy and infrastructure   35

Chapter 6: What was achieved?   43

Chapter 7: Sic evenit ratio ut componitur – again   77

Epilogue   81
Bibliography   85

About the author

Dr. Sir John Oldham qualified at Manchester Medical School in 1978 and worked in various teaching hospitals, culminating as a GP trainee in inner city Manchester. He was involved in setting up a GP Trainee forum in the North West. He joined Manor House Surgery, Glossop in 1983, becoming senior partner in 1988.

In 1992, he gained an MBA with Distinction from Manchester Business School; his dissertation was on Continuous Quality Improvement in Primary Health Care. The work in the practice led to him being asked to present a paper to the 1st European Forum on quality improvement in health care, and subsequent invitations to the US and Sweden. He was the first Briton to present a workshop at the US Forum on quality improvement in health care.

He was invited in 1997 by Don Berwick, CEO Institute of Health Care Improvement, to be on a national project group with the IHI in Boston, USA, looking at redesigning surgery systems in the US. This was being carried out using the Collaborative method which he then brought back to the UK. He first proposed a primary care collaborative in 1997 and ultimately this led to him being asked to create and head the National Primary Care Development Team which was launched in February 2000. This team operates several programmes including the national primary care collaborative. The aim is to create a critical mass of individuals in primary care, familiar with the techniques of improvement science.

In 2000, he received the OBE for services to patients, and 2003 was awarded a Knighthood for services to the NHS. He conducts workshops and presentations internationally. He does, however, still undertake regular clinical sessions in his surgery, usually two days a week.

*This book is dedicated to my wife, Julia,
my partner in all*

Preface

It was somewhat unnerving to be asked to write about my experience and knowledge of large system change and quality improvement. Firstly, it presumed I had sufficient of both knowledge and experience, and secondly presumed I could counteract the bad habit of a lifetime and write something coherent.

I have decided, therefore, to tell a story about creating large system change, out of which will emerge some key principles as I see them, together with practical hints and examples. The subject happens to be primary healthcare in England – but I hope the perception will be that the principles are generic and can be applied elsewhere.

For those who are seeking a text of encyclopaedic information on large system change and quality improvement, this is not the book for them. For those who would like to understand more about a method of how dramatic improvements in service provision were created for 31 million people in 38 months, whilst training and skilling front line staff in the science of quality improvement – then this book will be of interest.

However, I would first like to acknowledge the help and advice I have received. Initially, Don Berwick and IHI who gave me the opportunity to learn, Tom Nolan, Lloyd Provost and Paul Plsek who coached me, and all of the members, past and present, of the National Primary Care Development Team (NPDT) who helped deliver the vision. I would like to make particular mention of Ruth Kennedy and Guy Rotherham who were the first recruits to NPDT. I owe them much; very sadly Guy died suddenly in 2003 and I hope this is a fitting tribute to his legacy. In the production of this book, I am very grateful for the encouragement and advice of Paul Corrigan, and the expert editing of David Martin. Finally, thanks to the Civil Servants and Ministers whose courage in believing there was a different way enabled the story to commence.

Sir John Oldham
Glossop,
Derbyshire UK
May 2004

Foreword

If in 1998 John Oldham and his colleagues, launching the National Health Service's National Primary Care Development Team, had told me what they were about to accomplish, I would have publicly counselled them to be more cautious and privately thought them insane. To bring the benefits of technically difficult changes in scheduling and access, along with strong improvements in the reliability of scientifically-grounded medical care, to 31 million Britons in 38 months – is that not impossible? And, is intending it not just a little crazy?

I would have been wrong – seriously wrong. I would have been underestimating the assets and overestimating the risks. I would have been showing too little respect for John Oldham's extraordinary, creative leadership skills, authentic curiosity, vision, and attention to important details; too little confidence in the very methods of improvement and large-scale change that John was so carefully studying at the knee of many of my colleagues, like Tom Nolan, Mark Murray, Maureen Bisognano, and Lloyd Provost; too little intensity of commitment and willingness to invest of the UK Government and the leaders of the NHS to deliver on what the public most wanted from its health system. And, most of all, too little ambition to suit the immense potential of the National Health Service, itself, as one of the most courageous and compelling designs in all of human history for trying to assure that a nation receives, as a promise and a reality, the health care it deserves to have.

Right or wrong, I am an unrelenting fan of the NHS, not always for what it accomplishes, but always for what it is trying to accomplish. How fortunate John Oldham and his fellow citizens are to live in a nation that has set and continually affirmed a policy that its health care is a right, for all without exception, and free at the point of service! It is rhetorically correct (though my own nation still fails in the promise) to class health care among human rights. But it is, and will remain, a struggle to make that right a day-to-day reality. Health care is not a right in fact if it cannot be reached by anyone in need, if waits exceed tolerance and produce suffering. It is not a right in fact if it is defective, if it harms those who need its help, or if people cannot rely on it with absolute confidence.

This is the struggle – to perfect care – that the NHS will, so long as it remembers its mission, never stop. It is the struggle that, in its current form, motivates the "Modernisation Plan" of which the National Primary Care Development Team has been a central, inspiring part. The invitation that John Oldham accepted was to help make that Plan a reality, and to offer the next in a long and distinguished series of achievements to help the NHS be what it was created to be.

But, how? The scale of the challenge was immense. The main NPDT goal, "access to care", involved thousands of delivery sites – even if only General Practices were included – serving millions of people. "Access" referred to a complex quality of events occurring hour by hour in local settings everywhere in England – what service quality professionals would call "moments of truth". How could a vision and plan reach from Richmond House and Number 10 to the nation?

The answer to that question is, essentially, what John Oldham and his colleagues figured out, and then executed in a breathtakingly short interval. Indeed, I personally know of no improvement effort in any industry that has achieved in such a short time such a widespread and, frankly, technically difficult set of changes, with such stunning results, ever. Even the legends of modern quality improvement — the Japanese companies, the American manufacturers, the quality award winners – have involved, without exception, successes on a smaller playing field with fewer sites serving fewer people, maybe by an order of magnitude, than what the National Primary Care Development Team achieved. John and his colleagues may – I will be checked on this I hope – have achieved the largest deployed systemic improvement in modern history – not just in health care, but in history.

This neat, beautifully written book tells the story with John's characteristic good humour and originality. The elements he lists, drawing from the Romans, are three. He calls them:

1. the systematic transfer of knowledge
2. the creation of an environment that facilitated the uptake of ideas
3. a unified policy framework and infrastructure for spread.

It's a simple framework, but deceptively so. The "systemic transfer of knowledge" required a capable system for learning and coaching, one that could take the notions of Murray, Nolan, Provost, and others and make them accessible in real time to hundreds of busy practitioners and managers in hundreds of sites. Oldham, himself, accelerated this by becoming a learner par excellence. I saw him do it. He attended numerous Institute for Healthcare Improvement educational events, relentlessly sought the coaching of experts as his mentors, and blended uniquely the humility to ask more with the courage to try these methods himself and mould them to his use. His curiosity knew no bounds. (Even today I get phone calls from John asking me to review an idea of his or think with him about a problem. He is a searcher.)

As an "environment for the uptake of ideas", John began with The Institute for Healthcare Improvement's "Breakthrough Series" design for collaborative improvement, which started in the head of my colleague, Paul Batalden, in 1995 (I still have in my files Batalden's pencil drawing, which he handed to me at a Group Practice Improvement Network meeting in Detroit in 1994). The Breakthrough Series became, in Oldham's hands, a systematic plan for supported change in the UK, adapted and improved for that context. He added better measurement systems, better coaching, and more discipline. No one in the world today can lead a Collaborative better than John and his team can.

The "infrastructure" for spread and scale-up that John designed – a "wave" structure that used geometry more than arithmetic to gain spread in multiples – is a world-class innovation, providing other large systems, indeed nations, with a clear-headed model for leverage learning into change faster than anyone may have thought possible. Other leaders of change in health care have used "waves" to get traction, but no one has done it better than John Oldham and the NPDT.

To his native curiosity, his willingness to learn from others, and his courageous approach to adaptation and trial, John Oldham has added one more, essential, ingredient for success, and he has taught it relentlessly to his team, his NHS colleagues, his non-UK admirers (like me), and to anyone else who will listen. It is a little hard to describe, but I will call it, "A sense of the care". When the Nobel Prize-winning biologist, Barbara McClintock, was asked how she seemed to be able to work so well with corn (maize) as her prototype laboratory system – the one in which she made her most important discoveries – she replied that first she had to learn to "think like corn".

That's what John Oldham does. Working on care, he "thinks like the care". If you don't see that in this book, read it again. Deeply underpinning his work, a pedal point to every technique and theory, lies Oldham's knowledge and sense for what really happens when a doctor, nurse, or therapist sees a patient, when a human being who is trying to help meets a human being who needs help. Cutting through – unwilling to stoop to — the seductive cynicism about doctors, the sneers about government servants, the negative focus on defects and outrages, John Oldham heads straight for trust and hearts and good will. He deeply believes, and deeply respects, the premise that in the NHS good people are every day trying to help good people. That's why people listen to him. That belief – that respect – infuses every lecture he gives, every plan he cooks, and every fight he fights. If he seems intolerant of anything, it is of disrespect for the people who are struggling to make the NHS serve others, that is to say, most people. He understands the work. He "thinks like the care".

In this book, John Oldham and his team have taken the trouble to explain a brilliant system for improvement, a nearly unique accomplishment, in a way that others can study, emulate, and, as John himself has done, change and make their own. This is a system that transfers (and NPDT are transferring) to other public services. Enjoy it, and learn. As my good friend, Dr. Robert Waller, once told me: "Everything is impossible; until it's not." John Oldham and the National Primary Care Development Team have proven that as well as any change agents I have ever known.

Donald M. Berwick, MD, MPP
Institute for Healthcare Improvement
Boston, Massachusetts, USA

1

Background

▬ Introduction

A doctor wrote, "Over the years, initiatives have come and gone and passed me by. I was disillusioned and demoralised and on the point of early retirement. But my involvement in this work has moved from initial reluctance and scepticism to a rekindling of my enthusiasm and vocation. Thank you." Another said, "This has been one of the most positive things in my medical career"; another, "Staff are happier, patients are happier and doctors are less stressed".

In an environment where all the polls were showing that staff working in primary care were demoralised, and where difficult and potentially threatening negotiations were taking place between the British Medical Association and the Government about a new GP contract, what made these people feel that way? What was it that created such a profound change in them as individuals, and as a consequence in their performance and that of their organisations? Collectively they produced significant and sustainable improvement in care, yet without coercion. What phenomenon was at work?

The story started in 1987 with feelings of frustration about my own practice. We were decent people trying hard, but creating disease registers and doing a few audits was somehow not improving the range and content of the services we were offering. Overcrowded surgeries, queues, missing notes, loads of extras at the end of surgeries, unpleasant conditions and tension prevailed. It was quite depressing, and we started to question our capability. Then, in search of solutions, I came across an article about problems not being due to 'bad apples' or individuals most of the time, but about bad or flawed systems [1].

The article was written by Don Berwick of the Institute of Healthcare Improvement. It gave the insight as to why our conventional audits were insufficient – we were not understanding the totality of quality and the contribution, positive or negative, of all the stages of a process a patient experienced. This prompted me to search and learn more about some of the principles of continuous quality improvement (CQI) and process redesign [2]. Apart from my own reading I decided also that I wanted to seek out how other industries dealt with quality. At around the same time I took over the leadership of our GP partnership, and not having been trained in management, combined the two aspirations by undertaking an MBA at Manchester Business School. We built a new building for our practice and attempted to enact what I was learning about quality, looking at processes and involving everyone intimate to that process in the scrutiny and redesign; what I called microteams. These may be only 4–5 people since we were only a small organisation, but they met regularly for a limited period to examine a particular aspect of patient service. We made mistakes, went up some blind alleys but also achieved crucial early wins. Our operational outcomes and the service experiences of our patients were transformed. The practice gained national awards and met or exceeded national quality standards. We had our work accepted for presentation at the first European Forum on Quality Improvement in Health. It was with great surprise that on the back of the European Forum we received an invitation from Don Berwick to present at the US forum on quality improvement in 1995. We had entered the world family of improvement science.

At that time, being an enthusiast for the theories and practice of continuous quality improvement felt very much like being a Martian. But I gradually found that there were a few more Martians around in the UK, and kept in touch with each other by Peter Wilcock at Bournemouth University. The invitation to the US Forum made me realise that there was a planetary invasion. Through the work of a small cohort of people, improvement science gained a foothold in the National Health Service.

The network of which I was now part was a crucial formative experience, I think for us all in that grouping. Without the opportunity for contact and learning that it provided, the story would not have unfolded as it did. It was, and is, important to have these external opportunities to gain new knowledge, experience fresh thinking and receive support.

—— A brief history of quality improvement

It may be useful as a prelude to summarise very briefly the (quite complicated) history of concepts of 'product' quality.

The origins and development of quality improvement cannot be seen in isolation from the social and economic trends of recent history. The Industrial Revolution catalysed urban drift, a shift from individual craftsmanship to collective production, and the coalescence of people into organisations.

There was much variation in the quality of what was produced at that time but the sheer scarcity of new outputs or products meant that the approach to customers at that time was pretty much 'take it or leave it'. However, as more manufacturers started to produce a greater volume and wider choice of products for customers, they had to look for a competitive advantage either in the costs of production, or in quality, or in both, in order to be successful. This meant developing new ways of analysing and understanding work.

One approach that gained wide acceptance in the early 20th century was scientific management, or 'Taylorism' as it was called after its founder. The basis of Taylorism was a sad distinction between thinking (a management role) and doing (the worker's role). Workers' jobs were analysed, measured and fractionalised into their most basic elements. Manuals, rules, supervision and inspection governed their work. Those designing work processes were separate from those enacting them and innovation (the managers' prerogative as the process designer) was detached from the production line. In human terms the result for workers was often boredom, fatigue, minimum commitment and greater vulnerability to disruption, with little pride in or ownership of their work – and sometimes dodgy quality.

But a generally increased affluence in industrial societies fuelled rising expectations of quality amongst customers. Taylorism was incapable of a nimble response.

In the late 1920s and early 1930s there emerged the Human Relations approach, inspired in part by a famous series of studies at the Hawthorne works of the Western Electric Company of Chicago [3]. These showed that the motivation to work, productivity, and ultimately quality were correlated with the relationships between workers, and between workers and their managers or supervisors – in other words with human rather than mechanical or 'process' aspects of work. There was a confluence with other developing theorics on motivation, notably those of Maslow and Herzberg [4], which emphasised the importance of belonging, esteem and personal development in improving the experience and performance of work. The Human Relations movement laid the foundation for an understanding of the composition and functioning of teams.

Much of the work was centred around the relatively defined world of manufacturing. But even there the Human Relations advocates initially had little impact on the inheritance of Taylorism. The management of quality progressed from the detection of and re-working of aberrant products to more complex forms of quality assurance. But the emphasis remained on post-production detection, not intra-production prevention. Quality was for the quality department, not anyone else. Quality was an afterthought not a core belief, and certainly not a route to promotion.

Two American theorists, Deming [5] and Juran [6], drew on the Hawthorne research of the 1930s. They found that achieving quality by inspection was costly and counterproductive; that the fear invoked by inspection systems led to misinformation, with people providing not the true data which could highlight and help with the resolution of problems, but data they felt would keep the system quiet – 'feeding the beast', as it is sometimes called in the public services.

Yet Juran demonstrated that 'every process produces information on the basis of which the process can be improved'. Problems (and therefore opportunities to improve quality) are inherent in the complexity of work processes. Real improvement in quality depends on understanding and revising the processes themselves. Misinformation is inimical to quality improvement, and improvement must involve those who *really* understand the work process.

Tools and methods developed by Shewhart [7], including rapid cycle improvement techniques and control charts; and Ishikawa [8], including cause-effect diagrams, provided some ways of approaching an understanding of processes. Complete understanding, Deming argued, comes through dialogue that cuts across boundaries and requires a team approach. Natural work groups, focused on quality, are the engine rooms for problem solving and continuous improvement. The role of managers is then to create the climate, and provide the training and development, that permits people to do what is inherently within them – their best.

Theories of continuous quality improvement were slow to catch on and be put into practice in manufacturing industry. The best known and largest pioneer was Toyota. The approach revolutionised their company. For example, the changing of metal presses on a car production line was taking several hours. But by applying these techniques of involvement and analysis, Toyota reduced the changeover time to ten minutes on some lines.

Service industries, developing in the wake of increased prosperity and industrialisation, faced (and still face) a more immediate quality challenge: the 'workers' have a direct interface with customers. The nature of that contact, however brief, is what makes up the customer's mind about the quality of service and the 'product' – 'the moment of truth'. There will be many moments of truth in a day and many opportunities for success or failure. And getting it wrong has a substantial cost.

The Technical Assistance Research Programme (TARP) in Washington showed that a service business never hears from 96% of its unhappy customers, but when a customer has a problem, he or she will typically tell nine or ten others. Thirteen percent of unhappy customers will tell twenty other people.

On the other hand, if a complaint is handled well, TARP showed that 70% of customers will return; if it is handled both quickly and well this figure rises to 95%. These customers will also speak positively about the company with up to five other people.

These challenges lent themselves to the approaches developed by Deming, Juran and others. Modifications of continuous quality improvement methods began to appear in the service sector. The concepts of team working, a deep understanding of the needs of the customer, rapid feedback on problems and the empowerment of team members emerged as features of the best systems. It is not accidental that the 'lowliest' porter at a Ritz-Carlton hotel can organise you a room, a meal or a game of golf without sending you elsewhere, and has a mandated budget to help solve any problems.

Public services have followed the same trajectory as other service industries, but with perhaps a twenty-year lag. Even I can remember when it was pretty much 'take it or leave it' in most public services. The majority now tend to control quality by issuing standards and inspecting performance – Taylorism by any other name. Changes are occurring however, drawing in part on the experience of people in other service industries and driven by the demand that quality should be better in the public sector.

A customer's demand for improvement in quality is proportional to their expectation. That expectation was determined in the past by personal, direct, comparative experience; but the information revolution is changing the pace of that dynamic. People can now use the internet to find out what is possible and what others are achieving elsewhere. No service organisation, however small, can hide from that information-driven comparison. The requirement for improvement in order to survive is ever-increasing, and no longer just in the private sector.

Large service organisations can face particular challenges in this general consumer environment. How can they achieve the nimbleness that is necessary to adapt effectively and quickly? How can they take good practice and innovation from one place and emulate them in other places? How can they create a culture in which improvement effort is self-sustaining? How can they achieve large system change to transform overall performance and quality?

Quality and health

The traditional approach to quality in the health service has relied on the employment of good clinical professionals. There have been high barriers to entry, with initial examinations linked latterly to the notion of continuing 'fitness to practise'. Post-entry quality assessment approaches have evolved for work with individual cases or disease entities. Initially, such 'clinical audits' were random, 'personally dependent and complaint or research driven'. Over the years they have become more systematic and cyclical and linked to protocols for care. In several countries, including the UK, there have been attempts to unify such protocols in the form of national guidelines.

'Managerial' activity has been the second thread running through health service quality, usually linked to the creation of targets and the deployment of associated assessment or inspection methods. The foundation for this has been a *quality assurance* rather than *quality improvement* orientation.

Until perhaps ten or fifteen years ago, the 'quality of care' focus was generally on clinical care for individual patients. For years this notion was reinforced by the education of health professionals, which heavily emphasised the one-to-one relationship with patients and the individual accountability of clinicians, both in institutional and medico-legal terms.

The work of Donabedian [9] provided the insight that quality in health care is about more than just individuals, but about systems. He proposed a conceptual and analytical framework of *structure*, *process* and *outcome* and argued that a full analysis of structure and process should be carried out when seeking quality or outcome improvement. Although this approach does not necessarily promote nimbleness, it points in the right direction. But 'measuring is not enough, we must act'.

A growing appreciation that improvements in service quality depend on an understanding of systems has led naturally to a growing focus on the *teams* of people who contribute to the performance of systems. There is a huge literature on the way groups or teams work and the factors associated with success and frustration. The health services have put a lot of effort into building and sustaining teams (clinical teams, executive teams and Boards) and this has helped to create an environment in which improvement can be sought through system change.

However, two problems – themselves systemic – remain. Firstly, we have generally failed to see quality from the recipient patient's perspective rather than that of the clinician or the organisation, and as an issue for everyone to address. Patients have little understanding of and less patience with the 'system' demarcations and barriers that preoccupy and (on a bad day) amuse public servants.

Secondly, at the beginning of the 21st century it is still true to say that the inspection model holds greater sway than concepts of continuous improvement, and many professionals are still hooked on the belief that evidence-based care for a particular disease, with evidence preferably derived from double-blind controlled trials, is the sole benchmark against which health care should progress. Setting aside the fact that most double-blind trials go to elegant lengths to exclude patients with co-morbidity (i.e. more than one disease) when most patients have co-morbidity, this school of thought ignores the fact that the *system of delivery* for evidence-based care makes a massive difference too. In the words of Paul Batalden [10], "every system delivers exactly the results it is designed to give"; you may not deliberately design a system to give bad results, but a bad system will do so in any event.

In the UK the (excellent) concept of clinical governance is attempting to bring together individual accreditation and assessment with multidisciplinary organisational and inter-organisational activity to improve quality. Ultimately, however, such large system change has to be about empowering people to create the systems that maximise the results within the parameters of a clear strategic direction. Targets, measurement and inspection are not enough.

The story unfolds

Don Berwick and the IHI gave me tremendous opportunities to further my education. I was invited to take part in a group creating a programme to redesign "office practice" in the US. Participation in that was seminal. It exposed me to a method of spreading innovation and improvement to a number of organisations simultaneously; the IHI Breakthrough series. Excitedly, I talked to my Regional Health Authority in 1996 about undertaking a Breakthrough series back home – to no avail. The timing was wrong; there were recent NHS structural reorganisations (again) and the general election was approaching.

In 1997, the new Labour Government came to power in the UK. Its pledge to the electorate was to reform and improve public services, notably the National Health Service. The focus of media attention tended to be on the activity of hospitals – waiting lists for operations, waits at Accident and Emergency departments, waits to get out-patient appointments. In reality, hospitals only account for some 15–20% of total NHS activity, but the tangibility and greater glamour of that work made the stories easier copy.

Many political commentators felt that the Government had hooked its survival to change and improvement in public services. The Prime Minister,

Tony Blair, personally became very involved in setting the agenda for change, and in a series of private meetings, debating the mechanisms that could achieve that change. These discussions were fascinating and informed interchanges of views.

For a couple of years prior to the Government coming to power, I had been an advisor to the primary care division of the Department of Health. Two or three of us in that original Martian cohort of "quality improvers" had begun to develop relationships with the policy generating mechanisms of the NHS. It was clear from the election manifesto the scale of change envisaged was huge, and also clear that there were going to be opportunities in the decisions regarding 'how to'. Immediately after the election I put forward a paper to a senior civil servant outlining a proposal for achieving change in primary care. The suggestion was to create a small team that would seek to develop skills in continuous quality improvement in people and organisations in primary care. It would try to do this by engaging multidisciplinary groups in working on improving particular topics. Unsurprisingly the method I suggested was based upon the Institute of Healthcare Improvement Breakthrough series and an option of one of three topics presented. The name of the team was to be Service Quality and Organisational Development (SQuOD) team, to reflect the holistic approach. Or rather not to be. For the decision was made that organisational development was not included. This was an error which a year or so later was to be corrected, but in a way that led to fragmentation (from which we still suffer) by creating a different organisation to do that work. The reality is that you cannot separate the two; the lessons from industry (e.g. Hewlett-Packard) tell us that the bottom up approach to small teams delivering quality improvement is maximised by deliberative measures to develop people and organisations at a more macro level to help create the environment for sustainability and a culture of quality. Error two was mine – giving a choice of three topics to work on – the answer was all three!

The initial remit of the proposed team was to create measured improvement in access to primary care, the management of patients with established coronary heart disease, and the establishment of capacity and demand management systems between primary and secondary care. All participants would work on all three areas at the same time. Although seemingly disparate, these topic areas in fact covered the whole of a patient experience in primary care: access, the processes governing the management of an enduring illness within primary care, and the pathway between primary and secondary care for the 20% who went that route. Multiple disciplines were involved, small teams needed to deliver the improvement; in short the philosophy outlined by the pioneers of continuous quality improvement of looking at the whole process, was the one applied here.

The politics focused on the goals for the outcomes of the improvement in the specific topics. There was for us, however, an overreaching goal, a strategic intent for the whole of this activity – to develop a cohort of individuals that would create capacity and capability in primary care organisations for 'improvement science'. For that we needed to plan to create a critical mass, to impact on the whole of primary care. Before we got carried away by our own rhetoric, there was the small question of how we took the Breakthrough series method to produce large system change. The first principle was to see if anyone achieved large system change before, and an example, albeit quite old, came to mind.

2

Sic evenit ratio ut componitur

—— Introduction

It is amazing to think that around 100 AD the Romans had developed macro- and micro-economic systems, multi-storey buildings, piped water, sewage systems, central heating, heated baths, road systems, concrete buildings, theatres, and even cart parks. And these features were not just to be seen in Rome, but throughout the Roman Empire.

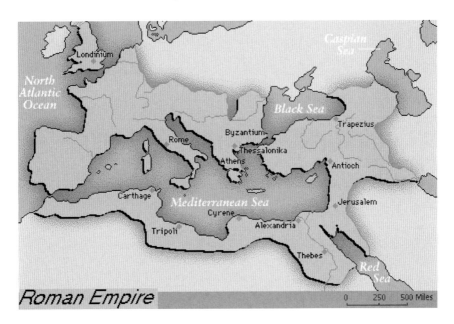

For example, the theatre in Orange in France, the baths in Bath in England, the aqueduct in Segovia in Spain, the mosaics in Caesarea in Palestine and countless villas, built in the same style, were all constructed at roughly the same time. How did they manage to get that knowledge and engineering skill spread throughout all that territory? Are there any lessons for us now when we are considering the management and particularly the change and improvement of large systems? The Latin phrase for it would be "Sic evenit ratio ut componitur", the meaning of which will gradually become apparent.

Their methods of disseminating information and skills can be précised (pace scholars of history) along the following lines.

Systematic transfer of knowledge

Skills and know how were transferred by personal teaching to apprentices and indentured servants. There was a formal basis for this in the shape of apprenticeship contracts, as illustrated by the Oxyrhynchis Papyrus of 66 AD in Roman Egypt (see below). Skilled apprentices and servants were in turn valuable and profitable as teachers in their own right. There is evidence in Cicero's letters of how a servant might teach his skills to others in the same household, but also be hired out to teach other households. Those skills could be in anything – building, engineering, joinery, even medicine. Apprentices and servants could sometimes work on their own behalf and even eventually buy their freedom, although a freed servant often had to pay a percentage of earnings to the original master. The important notion was that individuals could be taught skills, practice them under supervision and then independently, and in turn pass on their skills and knowledge to others.

Apprenticeship Contract; Oxyrhynchus Papyrus AD 66

Trypho, son of Dionysius, and Ptolomaeus, son of Pausirio, both parties being inhabitants of Oxyrhynchus, mutually agree that Trypho has apprenticed to Ptolemaeus his son Thoonis, who is not yet of age, for a period of one year from this day to serve him and perform all the duties given him by Ptolomaeus in connection with the weaving trade in all its branches as he himself knows it. The boy is to be fed and clothed during the whole period by his father Trypho, who is also to be responsible for all the taxes on the boy, on condition that Ptolomaeus shall pay him 5 drachmas a month on account of victuals and 12 drachmas on account of clothing at the termination of the whole period. Trypho shall not have the right to withdraw the boy from Ptolomaeus until the completion of the period, and if there are any days during it on which he fails to fulfil his obligation he shall produce him for an equal number of days after the period or shall pay a penalty of 1 silver drachma for each day; the penalty for withdrawing him within the period shall be 100 drachmas, and an equal sum to the public treasury. If Ptolomaeus on his part fails to instruct the boy thoroughly he shall be liable to the same penalties. This contract of

> apprenticeship is valid. Year 13 of Emperor Nero Claudius Caesar Augustus Germanicus, month of Augustus the 21st.

Creating an environment for the uptake of ideas

Knowledge was respected and prized during the Pax Romana, when Rome pacified large areas of the known world. Communications were improved and travel was both easier and safer. This facilitated the spread of ideas and techniques. People in the provinces who travelled perceived the gap that existed between what was possible and what they had locally. This had a pull-effect on the demand for ideas and know how. Rome was often depicted as a centre out of which knowledge as well as commodities flowed.

The Romans wrote important technical treatises, for example Vetruvius on architecture, Frontimax on aqueducts, and standard works on measurement. There were also encyclopaedic works covering various topics, both practical and theoretical, for example Pliny the Elder's *Historia Naturalis*. This written resource of expert knowledge became important during the expansion of the Empire, but there was limited access to the books, and they were written in Greek! No difference with some technical journals today, then.

With the limitation on the written word, there had to be another mechanism for conveying information, and narrative and story telling were it. Lectures and talks were regular events in the forums of towns and cities and were also one of the few means for an individual to advertise their skills.

> "...... like the exhibition of the physicians who seat themselves conspicuously before us and give a detailed account of the union of joints, the combination and juxtaposition of bones, and other topics of that sort such as pores and respirations and excretions. And the crowd is all agape with admiration and more enchanted than a swarm of children."

Poetry was also used. Nero's physician wrote several poems on antidotes to poisons: the unexpected medium facilitated retention of the facts. In the present day, Karl Weick [11] says people think narratively rather than argumentatively or paradigmatically.

Then there were the baths, an important part of Roman life in all parts of the Empire; a venue not just for bathing, but a social occasion; an opportunity for discourse and gossip – which, as it is today, was the knowledge network updating itself. The informal contacts made at the baths often led to further exchanges, the trade of ideas and the hiring and teaching of skills.

All these strands were woven together to create an effective environment for the uptake of ideas. Importantly, there was also in some places a recognition that to maximise and strengthen Pax Romana, the Romans needed to work *with* the culture of local populations in order to influence it (see below).

Policy framework and infrastructure for the spread of skills and knowledge

A further element was the existence of a unifying authority and policy framework which helped to create an infrastructure for the spread of skills and knowledge. The unifying authority was the Emperor (the term 'unifying' indicating the focus of power rather than a lack of opposition!). The Emperor set out general policies and provincial governors and procurators carried them out 'within the framework of local conditions and traditions'. In other words, broadly comparable policies and practices were implemented in different areas with a pragmatic attentiveness to particular local circumstances.

Many of these policies laid down requirements for specific developments and corresponding expectations about the skills that would need to be present in, or found by, an expeditionary force. The consequence of all this was a constant demand for the growth and distribution of knowledge and skill. The flow of knowledge was not just from the centre outwards. Reports from the provinces to Rome, and visits by provincial governors, ensured a two-way flow of information and knowledge. The office of the Roman Emperor thus became a repository of information that could transfer problem-solving capability from one part of the Empire to another. This is illustrated below by a letter from Pliny the Younger to the Emperor Trajan asking for an expert to be sent out to the province of Bithynia to help with a local engineering problem.

Letter from Pliny to the Emperor Trajan

... in the territory of the city of Nicomedia there is a very extensive lake, over which marble, produce and timber are transported by ship to the trunk road at modest cost and effort. Thence they are conveyed in wagons to the sea with great effort and expense, The Nicomedians therefore desire to connect the lake to the sea. This project requires many hands but these are available since the countryside and city are

> exceedingly populous. And one may definitely hope that everybody will support a project that will be profitable to all.
>
> It only remains for you to send, if you deem proper, a civil engineer to examine carefully whether the lake lies above sea level; the experts of this region maintain that it is about sixty feet higher. I find that there is in the same vicinity a trench which was cut by one of the kings. But as it is unfinished it is uncertain as to whether it was for the purpose of draining the adjacent lands or connecting the lake with the river, it is equally doubtful whether it is unfinished because of the intervening death of the king or abandonment of the hope of completing the project. But , you will forgive me being ambitious for your glory, I am urged on by this very fact and ardently desire that what kings merely began should be brought to completion by you.

In short, Rome had evolved a sort of knowledge management system.

The interaction between the provinces and Rome, the centre, was seen in Rome's increasing familiarity with the national resources of the various provinces, and in the provinces' awareness of the gap between what was possible and what people had locally. This flow of information, and the awareness of 'relative deprivation', stimulated innovation. For example, in building, local materials might not permit the straightforward transfer of technology: some inventions such as concrete, which depended on local volcanic deposits, could not readily transfer, but mortared rubble soon appeared as an alternative to achieve similar results.

So, policies set a framework which both pushed development and had a pull-effect on the demand for skills. The focus of power created broad similarity and a conduit for information and knowledge.

The army

In practical terms the Roman army played a massive role in the realisation of the framework. Expeditions had to include people with skills in engineering, building and land measurement. Some members of the army came with these skills from their civilian existence, but there was also training within the army, both formal and informal. The informal element just involved picking up the skills by working with someone who had them. Land improvement was an important army skill needed for laying out camps. Columella, a first century AD writer on agriculture, includes in his work a section on land measurement, not strictly his subject. He says he is a non-expert, but has included some instruction as a result of a request. Where did he get this non-specialist knowledge? From an inscription, we know that he was serving as a military tribune around 36 AD.

The army was not a self-enclosed unit: by necessity it interacted with local populations, and indeed they often provided the workforce for construction projects. Increasingly, legionaries themselves were from the provinces. This interaction, direct contact and practical experience helped spread skills and knowledge throughout the Empire.

Key principles

Although simplified and distilled, the features of Roman large system change were:

- the systematic transfer of knowledge
- the creation of an environment that facilitated the uptake of ideas
- a unified policy framework and infrastructure for spread.

I believe the same principles apply today to large system change. They are explored further in the next three chapters.

3

Systematic transfer of knowledge

Introduction

In most large organisations many people are often working on the same problem. In a small number of places people will have solved or partially solved the problem and have improved performance, but the rest of the organisation will probably remain ignorant of it: everyone ploughing the same furrow in their own way in their own time, and possibly never getting it right. Usually it is not some missing 'killer idea' or fact that holds things back, but the system and the processes that enact it. Don Berwick quotes the example that sixty years elapsed between the understanding by a naval Lieutenant that vitamin C prevented scurvy and the routine availability of citrus fruits on ships of the Royal Navy. Is the uptake of ideas random or does it follow a pattern? Can we speed it up systematically? Achieving large system change depends on understanding the answers.

Diffusion of innovation

The take-up of any new idea or product follows a well established (and researched) pattern. From the invention by *innovators*, a number of relatively risk tolerant people try it (*early adopters*), others follow once their confidence is enhanced by seeing the first users being successful (the *early majority*), then many more take it up knowing most people have done so (the *late majority*), with a residual smaller number who remain reluctant (*traditionalists*). The curve and labels were originally described by Everett Rogers [12]. Whilst in one sense too simplistic to describe the complex dynamic that governs the uptake of ideas, it nonetheless provides a pragmatic and graspable conceptual framework (see Figure 3.1).

What is apparent – and exponential – is that the effort to gain adoption is hardest up to around 20% of the population; beyond that the effort is easier. This concept of the *tipping point* was further explored by Gladwell in his book, *The Tipping Point. How Little Things Can Make a Big Difference* [13].

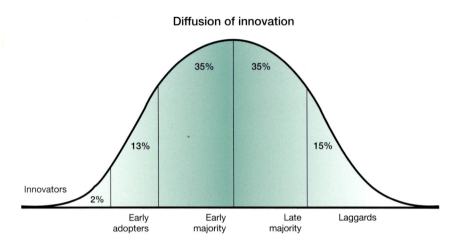

Figure 3.1: Rogers curve

His metaphor was a virus: that ideas, products, messages and behaviours spread like viruses do. He suggests that behaviour can be contagious and believes little changes can have a big effect. Amongst his rules of the tipping point, there are two which have particular resonance. Firstly, the 'stickiness factor': how problematic are the ideas or notion in the mind of the receiver. Secondly, and aligned to that, the power of content, which might be paraphrased as how the change is presented and its perceived value. The notion of the tipping point underpins the Collaborative method of spreading improvement, referred to previously as the IHI Breakthrough series.

Collaboratives

The definition of a Collaborative is:

> "An improvement method that relies on the spread and adaptation of existing knowledge to multiple settings to accomplish a common aim."

In other words it is the systematic transfer of such knowledge. How so? I will try and explain.

A Collaborative is designed to close the gap between what is known to be possible and what exists in most places. It relies upon the existence of substantive knowledge about what is possible, supported by examples of places where the knowledge has been applied to gain much better outcomes. A topic suitable for a Collaborative has to possess those characteristics.

A Collaborative is not:

- a set of conferences: meetings are working meetings
- a passive exercise: change is actively implemented
- a research project: the learning is dynamic and transferred as the Collaborative proceeds.

A Collaborative is a time-limited process consisting of a series of learning workshops at 3-monthly intervals, interspersed with action periods. During action periods, changes are implemented by the participating teams and measures common to the sites (in the National Primary Care Development Team version) are used to track progress. The basis for the workshops is exposure to examples of a new system, together with practical ideas that have resulted in those systems or flowed from them, and teaching on techniques of implementation. 'Master and apprentices' coming together with personal contact if you like, except that the relationship and information flow is much more equitable. For what is certain is that just as, at the start of a series of Collaborative workshops, the Collaborative organisers are sharing their current information, someone in a participating site will also have some useful knowledge that no one else is aware of and which adds to the collective enterprise (see Figure 3.2).

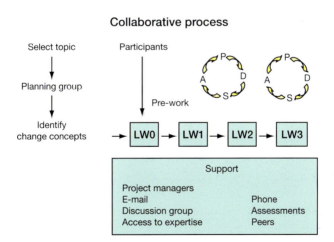

Figure 3.2: Schematic diagram of a Collaborative
Modified from Institute of Healthcare Improvement, Boston

> **Key features of a Collaborative**
> - *Expert reference panel*: examines examples where significantly better outcomes have been obtained and understands the anatomy of the new systems involved; from this, develops a set of change concepts underpinned by practical ideas of how to create a new system, shortening the discovery period for participants; this is their starting point and is in written up in the form of a Collaborative handbook.
> - *Learning workshops*: participants are exposed to examples of the new system in an enabling environment that encourages the sharing and testing of ideas and experience of what works and what doesn't; they are given techniques to lower the barriers to starting the change process, and time to plan what they will do in their own organisation.
> - *Action periods*: participants enact change in their own organisations; there is monthly feedback of results to all participants; successful ideas are shared, a network of information is created by the organising team.
> - *Support*: there are various levels of support – firstly that given by attendance and mingling at the workshops; secondly, the information fed back to the site by the Collaborative organising team each month; thirdly, on-site support by a facilitator and coach (in the NPDT version of a Collaborative); and the discussion group on a common website.

The learning at the (usually three) workshops is incremental. The interval between them can vary a little depending upon the topic. Where it is a tightly defined area and previous experience indicates it should be relatively easy for people to pick up the ideas, then the time interval can be seven to eight weeks rather than the usual three months. Conversely, for more difficult topics a fourth workshop might be added. The principle is to give participants sufficient time to build knowledge and test and measure improvements in their own setting. However, a Collaborative has a specific end point. Being time-limited is an important part of the method and contributes to the pressure to deliver results within an agreed period.

Setting a drumbeat for change with the monthly reporting of data from sites is a crucial element. Equally, returning the comparative analyses to participants within a short timeframe encourages learning and the drive for improvement. Quantitative data should be accompanied by text from the organising team which points up areas for further work and assists a cross flow of information with other participating sites. More operational details of the Collaborative method can be obtained from www.npdt.org "Introduction to Collaboratives" and Chapter 4.

Many Collaboratives are ends in themselves; 10–20 organisations coming together for 9 months or so to improve in a particular topic e.g. emergency care. This is perfectly valid. However, NPDT viewed the Collaborative method as the vehicle by which we would achieve the strategic objective of creating improvement science capacity and capability in primary care organisations. The Collaborative provided the means of systematically transferring knowledge, but also a mechanism for creating a cohort of individuals to become involved themselves in the future transfer of the acquired knowledge. The taught become the teachers.

Plan Do Study Act

A pivotal notion of the Collaborative method is how to implement change rapidly. This principle is enshrined in the *Plan Do Study Act* cycle. This model, developed by Langley and colleagues [2] is the cornerstone for getting teams going. Enacting a series of small cycle changes enables the rapid establishment of the 'change principle' for a new system. The full implementation of the change principle, the basic anatomy of the new system, is the transformation sought.

The model for improvement used in a Collaborative is based on the observation that organisations that make rapid improvement do so by answering three basic questions about the planned change, and that they are able to use small-scale tests of change that are based on the answers given to the questions to deliver the desired improvements.

The questions are:

- what are we trying to accomplish?
- how will we know if a change is an improvement?
- what changes will we make that will result in an improvement?

Making improvements in services means changing things. Change can seem threatening or overwhelming for busy people doing demanding work. The PDSA method is a way to break down change into manageable chunks and test each small part to make sure that things *are* improving and no effort is wasted.

PDSA stands for Plan Do Study Act. It is a model for testing ideas that you think may create an improvement. It can be used to test ideas for improvement quickly and easily based on existing knowledge, research, feedback, theory, review, audit etc, or practical ideas that have been shown to work elsewhere. It uses simple measurements to monitor the effect of changes over time. It encourages starting with small changes, which can

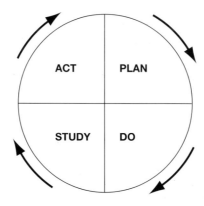

build into larger improvements in the service through successive quick cycles of change.

> **PDSA is**
> - a common sense approach to change and improvement
> - quick and simple
> - do-able
>
> **PDSA is not**
> - complicated
> - difficult
> - gimmicky

It works. The PDSA cycle has been used for decades as an effective tool for improvement and is still going strong. The method is well established and validated and is particularly suited to small, dynamic organisations like general practice. It is an extremely practical, common sense-based approach that is easy to understand.

> **Step 1: Plan**
> Identify what change you think will create improvement and then plan the test of the change. What is your objective in introducing the change? It is important to establish the scope of the change to be introduced, and how you are going to collect information about the differences that occur. How will you know whether the change made has 'worked' or not?
>
> The change should be capable of bringing about differences that are measurable in isolation. A major change could be broken down into

smaller more manageable 'chunks'. Once the actual change to be introduced has been agreed, the following questions should be asked:

- what would we expect to see as a result of this change?
- what data do we need to collect to check the outcome of the change?
- how will we know whether the change has 'worked' or not?
- who, what, where, when?

Step 2: Do
Put the plan into practice. Test the change by collecting the data. This stage involves carrying out the plans agreed in Step 1. It is important that the 'Do' stage is kept as short as possible, but note that there may be changes that should only be measured over longer periods. Record any unexpected events, problems and other observations. Start analysing the data.

Step 3: Study
Review and reflect. Complete the analysis of the data. Has there been an improvement? Did your expectations match the reality of what happened? What could be done differently?

Step 4: Act
Make further changes or amendments, and collect data again, after you have decided what worked and what did not. Carry out an 'amended' version of what happened during the 'Do' stage and measure any differences. It is important to take the learning from the cycles into account in your next cycle of change, so *act differently* as a result of your review.

PDSA cycles can build on each other as small changes lead to other changes or bigger changes, and so on and so on. PDSA cycles reduce the difficulties in getting started. Testing small changes sequentially means that design problems can be detected and amended earlier rather than later, saving huge amounts of effort being put into massive change which has to be revised. However, it is sequencing a cycle that institutes the larger change.

As with everything there are tips to make PDSAs work better:

- Keep it simple and very specific.
- Keep it small and manageable to start with – massive projects can be broken down into a number of small, quick PDSA cycles.
- Cycles should happen quickly – think in terms of a week not a month!
- There is no *wrong* answer, but if you find something that works, use it.
- Copy and adapt other people's ideas if you think they may be useful.
- Many make the error of filling in Plan Do Study Act columns at the outset; you can of course only complete Plan and Do until the cycle has run.

The Collaborative method and large system change

A key feature of the Primary Care Collaborative operated by NPDT was building in the concept of spread from the outset. We did not wish this to be an initiative that came and went, but a commencement of a movement for change that would be sustainable. The next two chapters relate how we attempted to stimulate the environment necessary for the change, and created the strategy and infrastructure to achieve the large scale we required.

4

Creating an environment that facilitates the uptake of ideas

Introduction

If I may paraphrase Parker Palmer, methodology can systematically disengage us from the power of the heart. Yet it is the coalition between hearts and minds which drives improvement to new levels. My early experience of the collaborative methodology was that perhaps the teaching of methods and techniques was insufficiently balanced with an understanding and encouragement of the social and psychological aspects of change.

If we were to achieve the strategic objective of creating capacity and capability for quality improvement in primary care organisations, then we had in a sense to develop a *movement*. We would need people themselves to feel motivated and empowered to take the ideas forward, to desire to perpetuate and spread them. The requirement on us was to try and understand the principles behind these social and psychological elements of change, and design them into our processes.

Individuals, culture and change

The starting point is a return to the Rogers curve for the diffusion of innovation as a structure of convenience (whilst accepting its academic limitations) (see Figure 4.1).

The labels given to the various groupings under the curve are often erroneously attributed to personality traits: 'He or she is a classic innovator, or a die-hard laggard'. The reality is that each and every one of us is a member of each of those groups at different times. The factor that changes is not our personality but the understanding that we are being asked to adapt, and our personal response to that particular idea on the day.

The other mantra is 'resistance to change'. Paul Plsek [14] talks instead, more sophisticatedly, about 'attractors to status quo', what it is that makes someone wish to stay where they are. The valuable corollary of this view is that by understanding what the attractors might be to *new* ideas, and the

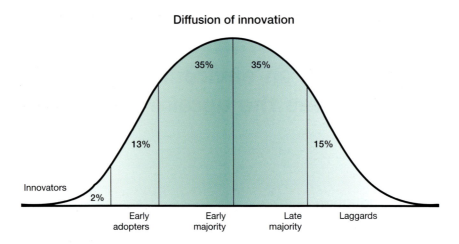

Figure 4.1: Rogers curve

perceived *negatives* of the current situation, the barriers to change can be reduced.

As an individual therefore, our position on the Rogers curve is the resultant of an equation: anxiety about change versus anxiety about the status quo. Conventional collaborative methodology focuses on identifying early adapters and speeding their acquisition of the change. Our belief was that amongst the participants we would be faced with people at every point on the spectrum. Our job would be generally to reduce the anxiety about change, so moving the position of individuals on that curve, whichever position they originally occupied. For that we needed to understand the elements of the equation (anxiety about change vs anxiety about the status quo), what I term the *personal risk equation*.

There are four elements to this. Firstly, the *characteristics of the new idea(s)*, the features which will shape our response to them:

- relative advantage – what evidence is there that if I accept these ideas things will improve?
- compatibility – how compatible is the idea with the current structure, organisational values and culture?
- simplicity – can the idea be simply described or is it quite complex to understand?
- testability – can I test whether the idea might work for me, or if I make the change is it difficult to reverse?

- observability – if I make a change and adopt the ideas, will I see a difference or is it 'jam tomorrow'?

The second element to the personal risk equation is whether the *ideas are aligned with, or challenge, my personal values*. At its most extreme, no sanction of performance management can be greater than the injury of conspiring against your own beliefs.

Thirdly, will there be an *actual or perceived impact on my lifestyle or status* if the ideas are adopted?

And finally, is there an impact on me *financially*?

Although as individuals we do not consciously go through this process of analysis, I feel it is a deconstruction of what we do intuitively.

Further analysing the ideas in this way *from the perspective of the person you are wishing to encourage to change* gives insight into the main attractions of the idea and the elements with the potential for heightening anxiety. It also allows the shaping of the explanation of the ideas in a way that has the best harmony with the organisational culture. This is not unlike the way in which, during Pax Romana, the Romans sought to work 'with the grain' of differing cultures throughout the Empire whilst retaining a unity of purpose.

There is a parallel with conveying ideas in another arena, that of education. One theory of education defines the stages traversed by an adapting or learning individual as awareness, pre-contemplative, contemplative and absorption. This can be re-stated in terms of reducing anxiety to change:

- Awareness: knowing the possibility of success exists
- Pre-contemplative: hearing about someone who has achieved success
- Contemplative: knowing someone who has achieved success
- Absorption: seeing results in your own organisation.

See Figure 4.2.

Collective position and change

Up to now we have been discussing the response of individuals to new ideas. However, we wish to make large-scale change and must therefore transpose the individual-level principles to the collective level of the collaborative method. A key element in that transposition is shaping the style and substance of communications, and this will be addressed in a later section. The other main element is taking the principles into account in

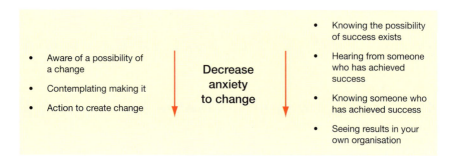

Figure 4.2

designing the three learning workshops and their agendas so as to give people confidence and reduce anxiety about change (see Figure 4.2).

At the initial 'orientation event' participants are made aware of the possibility of change and the results achieved by others. This is a variation on the original IHI collaborative method. It also allows the ventilation of any angst or grievance as to why a team is anticipating, and allows the clarification of mutual expectations. For example, making it clear that data submission is the nutrition for the collaborative – that is what allows the organising team to create the network amongst participants. At the first 'learning workshop' proper they hear directly from people who have already achieved success. Between the first and second learning workshops considerable effort is put in by the Collaborative organising team to identify and coach those participants who seem to be adopting the ideas most quickly. So, by the time the second learning workshop comes around some of the participants themselves will be presenting their success (giving confidence to other participants by *knowing someone* who has recently achieved success).

Between the second and third learning workshops the aim is to identify exemplars of progress in each site. This is with an eye to the spread of the work to organisations not attending the workshops, but connected locally to the participating sites. They will have the same initial spectrum of views and opinions about the ideas, but knowing someone locally who has achieved them will give confidence about making changes.

During the workshops themselves, the Collaborative organisers will meet at the end of day one (in a two-day workshop), or half way through a one-day workshop, to analyse where the 'stickiness' may be, and adjust the emphases in the subsequent sessions to try and address that. Students of knowledge management will perceive echoes of that discipline.

Respecting and conveying knowledge

Curiosity and a requirement for knowledge characterised the Roman culture, as did a desire to transfer or share it with friends. Respecting knowledge is also a priority for the Collaborative approach to large-system change. There are people out there with solutions and bright thoughts we are just not aware of. The collaborative commences with a sharing of current knowledge but is constantly acquisitive of further knowledge from participants as their practice and experience evolve. The pool of examples and information on a given topic is greater at the end of a series of workshops than at the beginning. For this to happen effectively, the transfer of knowledge has to be systematic, and the style and tone of the workshops have to facilitate openness and honesty, about setbacks as well as successes. This is why it is so vital that such activity, where error is 'okay', is perceptually distanced from the performance management structures and cultures of the participating organisations. That sentence is worth repeating.

The systematisation focuses around the data and information gathered monthly by the Collaborative organising team. They become aware of what is going well and what is not; who has progressed and who has not; the new ideas and ways of implementing them that have emerged. From this 'helicopter' perspective they can proactively assist the network of information flows, feed the good examples into the workshops and even put sites in direct touch with each other.

We have seen that the relative paucity of written material pushed the Romans into using narrative as a means of conveying information. Today we have multiple means of communicating and accessing information, yet narrative and story-telling stories remains one of the most powerful. A learning workshop format will normally involve a plenary session setting the learning agenda crisply, with parallel breakout sessions about practical examples in more depth: people telling their stories. During the workshops there are also scheduled times for the teams from each site to discuss and plan their own changes, and then relate their experiences.

For multidisciplinary and (more acutely) multi-agency teams, we have found (through getting it wrong!) that structured narrative is a prerequisite to enabling attendees nominally from the same site to begin to function as part of a coherent team at the workshops. The structured narrative follows the lines of David Cooperrider's *Principles of Appreciative Inquiry* [15]: telling a story of an incident where things worked well, identifying what was happening that made it work well, conjuring up a joint vision of how those conditions could occur more readily, and implementing that vision. The trick is then to link that approach to the complementary PDSA rapid change cycle. The result is synergistic.

─── **Communication**

Communication is the lubricant for improvement and change, and for updating the knowledge in information systems. I would like to tackle this on three levels: firstly the shaping of what is communicated, secondly the handling of communication within a collaborative, and thirdly the mechanisms for communicating to others external to the collaborative as a means of increasing involvement.

In an earlier section, I described the Personal Risk Equation and its components, which create a tension that determines the balance between anxiety about change and anxiety about the status quo. An element in that equation was the characteristics of the ideas being put forward. I suggested they contributed to an appreciation of the ideas' strengths and also of causes for concern. This analysis was undertaken from the perspective of the people you wish to adopt ideas. The 'net' appreciation of a particular set of ideas will vary amongst different groups of people e.g. production managers vs the market department, clinicians vs health care managers, teachers vs local education authority officials. So it is important to understand the likely response of different segments of the population you wish to communicate with and to communicate accordingly and repeatedly. In the words of someone whose name I do not recall, this may mean "saying it seven times in seven ways". Let me try and illustrate with the example of improving access to a GP's surgery from the perspective of a GP. The emphases in their perceptions would be distinctively theirs.

- *Relative advantage*: we know from examples that there are advantages in reducing aggression, improving the working lives of doctors and receptionists, and increasing the level of patient satisfaction; but these advantages would not be perceived initially and the evidence may not be believed.
- *Compatibility*: improving access could be seen as compatible with improving health care by some GPs, but the majority would find the concepts counter-intuitive. The fear would be that demand would escalate.
- *Complexity*: relatively straightforward ideas when presented correctly.
- *Testability*: very testable and would be seen as such.
- *Observability*: if implemented, change could be seen relatively quickly.

The messages we communicated would need to point up the advantages, whilst at the same time addressing the most potent apprehension i.e. that already busy surgeries will be overwhelmed – which is not in fact the case. Those who have already made the change find surgeries run more smoothly, that there is less hassle, and that doctors, receptionists and patients regard the new system as substantially better. This message is delivered right from the outset, with the initial invitation to be part of the Collaborative, and then reinforced at the workshops, in booklets and by other communication means. Whilst the illustrated message is only a small part of the total thrust of communication about the proposed changes, it serves to demonstrate the need for planned and controlled communication and how this assists in the overall aim of engaging people to test the change in their own environment.

It is important to remain tuned in to how your promotion of the ideas is being received. For example, we hit two particular problems. Initially we used the phrase "working smarter not harder", which at first seemed to resonate but was soon used so widely as a kind of mantra that it began to grate with people, lost meaning and any real communication value. It was dropped. Secondly, whilst it is not the purpose of this text to describe the new system of access that was proposed, the fundamentals were around redesigning operations to pull work forward and to alter how it was handled. The phrase "doing today's work today" was coined. Unfortunately, some of the early converts took that literally and prevented people booking appointments in advance! We were not swift enough in detecting this, and some replication in other practices had taken place. Although corrective measures were taken, it was a bit like the collaborative version of Japanese knotweed, and the legacy lasted quite a while.

Underpinning this sort of headline message, which can help frame the ideas and set a tone, are a wealth of practical details which also have to be communicated. It is always worth remembering that learning styles differ: some people prefer to read, others to listen to formal inputs and take notes, others to access information electronically. Most people like to talk informally, however, and whilst Roman baths are in short supply the informal exchanges at the workshops, at lunchtimes or during the evenings, are an invaluable and integral part of the process. Enabling them to happen in timetabling events is a task for the Collaborative organising team.

We are, however, interested in large system change, and for that we need to communicate beyond the confines of workshops and their participants. Whether it is wished to recruit people into the work within the vicinity of existing participants or to attract new sites, raising awareness is the first step (recall: knowing the possibility that success exists). Again, a variety of means is best, from articles in the relevant media to targeted leaflets or letters, video, and awareness raising days about the topic, all using some of the examples created in the Collaborative.

Raising awareness proactively is one thing, but you also need to have in place a system for responding to unsolicited interest. This relates to the Collaborative's management infrastructure, which is discussed in the next chapter. However, it is worth bearing in mind that the more personal the response, the more likely you are to shape behaviour and gain involvement. But there is also a desirable sequencing of personal contact, which tends to be received most positively after prior raising of awareness and the passing of information in conventional, less personal forms.

In parallel with proactive campaigns and managed responses to individuals, it is important in seeking large system change to identify opinion leaders who will promote the change for you. There may be groupings or networks who would not receive the message well from the Collaborative organisers, but who may from others. There may of course be opinion leaders who are at different points on 'the curve' and it makes good sense not solely to engage with the converted. It is better to recruit the influential but unconvinced as uncommitted observers than to have them outside the tent doing the proverbial.

Finally, and self-evidently, timely communications with the sponsors of the large system change are crucial. They may need ammunition to gain continued corporate support. Credibility though is all: only say something when you've something to say, and only tell it as it is and not as you would like it to be.

━ Back to the story

The decision had been made about a name. A National Primary Care Development Team would be created to operate a Primary Care Collaborative. There would be three topics or development areas as previously outlined and all participants would address all three. In fact, too *good* a job had been made of describing the philosophy behind a collaborative and the concept of a tipping point (20% on board as implementers) was well understood. But could that proportion of the population be achieved in twelve months asked the sponsor (the Department of Health)? I thought two years, but we compromised on eighteen months.

As with many decisions in large corporate bodies, there is a lag time to the moment of decision, but once it has been made the sponsor pressure is for everything to happen soonest. There was also a different and, because of my own naiveté, unexpected other pressure that came out of raising awareness amongst stakeholders (in other parts of the Department of Health and the NHS for example) about what was going to happen. Everyone wanted their pet topic included: "perhaps you could do a bit with diabetes", or whatever. It was important to resist this pressure, as it would be for others embarking on large system change. There is a price to pay for that resistance, but focus is important in order to produce the results which gain wider engagement and, hopefully, sustainability.

I negotiated to take three months out of my practice to set the team up and recruit the initial members. And so it was that in January 2000, there were four of us in a room, one of whom was my PA, Gill Bell, and the others, Ruth Kennedy and Guy Rotherham, both with excellent management skills but no knowledge of collaborative methods. I say this not in any sense to understate their abilities, but to underscore that what happened subsequently was more to do with getting the right people and then teaching the skills and techniques than trying to find non-existent, off-the-shelf, perfectly equipped recruits. We now needed to create the structure to deliver.

5

Strategy, policy and infrastructure

Introduction

In an earlier chapter I described how the Romans had overarching imperial policies, setting a strategic framework which had a pull effect on the demand for skills. These policies were interpreted 'according to local conditions and traditions'. The Roman army and its legionnaires played key roles in delivering on policies and ensured their empire-wide adaptation.

Most large organisations operate under a strategic umbrella, a set of policies intended to move the organisation in a certain way. The NHS is no exception and in late 2000, the NHS Plan was launched by the Government as the framework for reforming the health service. It envisaged care redesigned around the patient, a "seamless" service, and an emphasis on the quality of patients' experience and outcomes. The ability of the various parts of the NHS – a truly massive organisation – to deliver these policies would depend in part upon their aptitude in quality improvement work. The Government's policies therefore had a pull effect on the requirement for improvement skills, and set the environment within which the Collaborative would operate.

As we have said, the Collaborative was simply the vehicle for achieving the strategic intent of creating capacity and capability in primary care organisations for the use of quality improvement methods. We needed to develop a cohort of individuals, legionnaires if you like, who themselves possessed the skills. Many of the skills in Roman times were embedded in local populations precisely because some legionnaires were recruited from those populations and returned to live in them. Sustainability, we hypothesised, would come from developing that cohort of individuals within the primary care organisations themselves. This contrasted with alternative approaches in other parts of the NHS, aiming to driving the same agenda, who tended to suck people out of the system to create large central teams to 'do it' to NHS organisations, as it were from the outside.

Primary care

It is necessary to digress at this point to explain briefly, to those who are unfamiliar with it, the structure of primary care in England. The front line delivery units of primary care are in the vast majority of cases the practices of primary care doctors (GPs). These are most frequently grouped as three or four physicians in a practice, although there is a trend towards larger practices. GPs are mostly independent contractors, but work within the local organisational framework of a Primary Care Trust (PCTs) covering a population of around one to two hundred thousand. PCTs evolved from slightly smaller organisations, Primary Care Groups (PCGs), which were in the majority when the Collaborative began work. There were around 310 PCGs at the beginning of 2000, with some 20-25 practices in each.

The application process to become a site on the Collaborative was three times over-subscribed.

The infrastructure

The considerations in designing the programme and its structure were:

- the aim of achieving a critical mass of 20% of organisations (the Rogers curve)
- the need to create a cohort of individuals with quality improvement skills
- the importance of planning the 'spread' of learning, know-how and commitment from the outset.

Achieving the tipping point was simply a question of mathematics. Eighty PCG/Ts was on the right side of 20% of the country. The tipping point within a PCT representing 20% of their constituent practices, would be around five practice teams.

We wished to try and create a system where sequential learning would occur in the hope that change would be accelerated by the spread of news about the earliest participants. This, and the logistics of numbers that could be coped with at learning workshops, shaped the pattern.

We decided upon four waves with 20 PCG/Ts in each wave and a four to five month stagger between their starts. Some fifteen people from each PCG/T would be participants at the workshop representing the five core practice teams, together with some PCG/T managers – around 350 per workshop.

There were two elements in creating a cohort of individuals with skills in improvement methods. Firstly, each PCG/T site would establish a full-time project manager. They would be employed by the PCG/T, but trained by NPDT and obliged to take advice from NPDT on how to operate the Collaborative locally. Their responsibilities were coaching the core practices, ensuring data submission, creating local awareness and recruiting practices for spread. We found their competence was a key success factor for the sites, and the prime competency was people skills – the improvement techniques themselves could be taught.

The second element to be considered in creating a cohort was the untapped talent to be discovered amongst the participants attending the workshops. As part of the Collaborative process, good practical examples were created and people from those practices demonstrated both to others in the same wave and to subsequent waves what could be achieved. Within that group were a smaller number of individuals who demonstrated particular interest or talent for quality improvement who could be given wider exposure and coaching. For some, this entailed acting as "clinical chairs" for future waves of the Collaborative.

There were also two aspects to planning the spread. The task was to gain greater penetration of practice teams within the existing sites. This has been alluded to and was the task of the project managers in the sites. They received bi-monthly training centrally in, for example, coaching and group skills, process flow and redesign, data management, communication and spread techniques, improvement science etc. They were encouraged to, and did, create a network between themselves, swapping ideas and sharing problems, and they had a bespoke area on the website to facilitate this.

The four waves ran consecutively with a three to four month overlap. In the first year the core practices attended the workshops and in the second they were involved in consolidating their work (some using the methods for other topics) and assisting in local and national spread. Throughout the two years of a wave's participation, the core practices, and the spread practices as they came on stream, supplied monthly data which created the aggregate improvement measure for the Collaborative. By the end of 2001, some 1500 practices covering one million patients were engaged with the Collaborative as a result of this activity.

The second part of the spread plan was more ambitious: how to reach all PCG/Ts not yet involved. It was recognised that if the work was to be spread so widely and be sustainable, many individuals would have to acquire skills in improvement science and that the responsibility for operating the collaborative methodology could not reside solely with the original NPDT. The idea was to take applications from sites on the first three waves (the fourth had not completed when we needed to do this) to become NPDT Centres in their own right. The centres were to be geographically distributed around the country and operate more localised Collaboratives. The sites for these NPDT Centres were selected PCTs within designated geographical "patches". Between them the NPDT Centres would cover all the remaining PCTs in the country. Facilitators were established in each of these remaining PCTs and linked to the relevant NPDT Centre; they were the equivalents of the project managers in the national waves (see Figure 5.1).

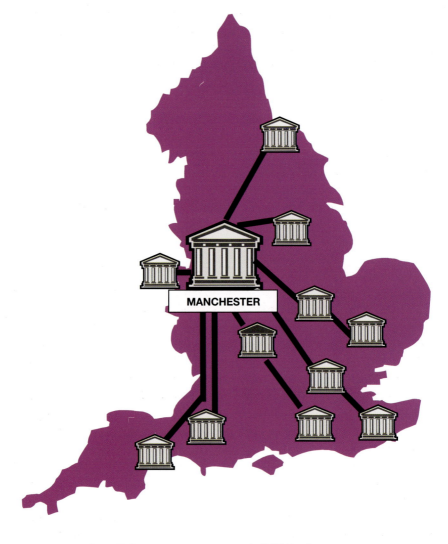

Figure 5.1: NPDT Centres covering each PCT in the country

The applications were evaluated and eleven sites chosen; each Centre would consist of around four people who would be the organising team for the local Collaborative. However, they could call on and use the existing project managers and exemplars from the national waves to assist in their task.

By this time a feeling of 'family' had begun to develop. The establishment of an NPDT Centre was a formal arrangement. There was a contractual agreement between NPDT and the PCT where the centre was placed. This stipulated that the Collaborative had to be operated on NPDT lines, using our materials, and the Centre would be accountable to NPDT for its performance and financial probity. Equally, it outlined the training and support available to the Centre team from the NPDT. A substantial part of the training of facilitators was operated centrally by NPDT to reduce dilution.

There was considerable disquiet at this plan from sponsors of the collaborative, including high levels of Government. Having seen the results of the national waves, their preference was to run national waves 5, 6, 7, 8 etc. The disquiet translated into a fair amount of pressure. Any change produces anxiety and large system change can generate large anxiety. However, the main sponsor imperative was rate of improvement and spread. Our plan demonstrated that, effectively, twenty-two waves of the collaborative could be completed within eighteen months. We were given the go-ahead.

Leadership and organisational development

No large system change can occur without the concurrent development of leadership and organisations. The original name for the NPDT was intended to be the Service Quality and Organisational Development Team (SQUOD), reflecting our desire to run work, in parallel with the practice-oriented work, for the management of PCG/Ts in the sites on the Collaborative. This would have been the most sensible arrangement and I would advocate those contemplating large system change to be inclusive in this aspect of their thinking. However, we were restricted by and large to assisting practices with their development as organisations through the mechanism of seeking practical improvement on a specific topic. In addition there was an opportunity for practice staff to be involved at a later stage in attaining higher level quality improvement skills through a course operated from the NPDT centres (on-stream at the end of 2003).

Developing leaders per se, we took not just to be leaders in formal positions, but also those who would wish to retain their current clinical role yet be able to act as influencers and represent NPDT on occasions. From the national waves we identified a number of people to whom we gave further development opportunities, and provided additional expertise for the NPDT Centres. These "NPDT affiliates", as they are known, had the opportunity to learn more about improvement techniques, and gain a wider perspective on national and international activities. This was accompanied by understanding in greater depth their own skill and personality traits.

So far we have eighty trained project managers from the national waves, eleven NPDT centres with staff learning and running Collaboratives, and two hundred facilitators in PCT. At the time of writing, after the first phase of the NPDT Centre Collaboratives, there are 4900 practice teams engaged, covering some thirty one million patients. The NPDT affiliates will be spearheading an initiative which will offer a higher level of knowledge about quality improvement science to those who wish to seek it. It has been developed with Tim Wilson from the Royal College of General Practitioners; acronymed QUiSP, it will operate from each NPDT centre. The NPDT Centre Collaboratives will also be the source for the next generation of NPDT affiliates. 100 of them are to be selected to take part in an 18 month personal development initiative. This builds on the learning from the first phase for affiliates and will include exposure to leading edge thinkers, policy makers, and learning about concepts of organisational behaviour and design.

Collaborative Organising Team

Reference has been made on several occasions to the 'Collaborative Organising Team', whether for the NPDT national waves or the NPDT Centre Collaboratives.

Rather than define exact structures, perhaps with the exception of the need for a Chair, it is probably more useful to outline the tasks that have to be performed. Each Collaborative wave does need a figurehead in the person of the Chair. He or she should have credibility with participants in terms of their existing knowledge and experience. Their main roles are to front the workshops, chair the meetings of the Organising Team during and between the workshops, and represent the Collaborative to a wider audience.

There is also an overall co-ordinating role to ensure that day to day management happens appropriately and shapes the agendas for the learning workshops. This is usually linked to monitoring overall results and identifying and responding to the training and development needs of the rest of the Organising Team. Events need to be organised, not only in terms of constructing the agenda and checking out the content of presentations, but also in terms of the logistics of finding venues and monitoring their responsiveness and quality. Ensuring data reporting and feedback on PDSAs, and assembling global statistics, are crucial, as indeed is the front-end response from administrative staff – they are the Collaborative's shop window.

This is how we translated these requirements for the original NPDT structure:

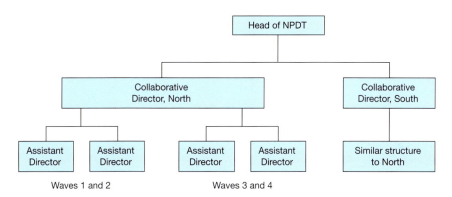

This team at one stage was running learning workshops every four weeks. Once the NPDT Centre criteria were established and the national team were less involved in running the workshops, the structure was adjusted to reflect the new arrangements. The collaborative operating teams were now in the field, and the national team had a coaching and monitoring role – and was also expanding its work into other areas with other agencies. These details need not concern us but the principle of continuous assessment and adaptation is the important notion for organisational operation and structure when generating large system change. This is an alien concept in many bureaucracies that are large systems, and creates its own tensions.

── The legions gather

In this chapter, I have described how there was a systematic approach to creating an infrastructure for improvement using the collaborative as the vehicle for change and as a treasure chest for talent. The development of individuals and their skills through direct personal contact and learning was key. Many "served their apprenticeship" to contribute their own innovations and improvements to the methods, which not only added to the pool of knowledge but enhanced sustainability.

And so, what were the results of all this activity and planning?

6

What was achieved?

—— Introduction

The primary purpose of this document is to convey some of the thinking and the human and organisational issues involved in applying improvement science to practical challenges in the public service sector. In particular we have looked at the PDSA approach as a way of achieving improvements through rapid cycles of 'experiment', and the spread of change know-how through collaborative methods.

However I think it might be a little frustrating for readers not to hear how the National Primary Care Team actually got on and this Chapter sets out some of the results we have achieved. For those who are interested, the detail of some of the change principles employed for the topics are listed, together with some of the examples created through the Collaborative. The final section shows how the process has helped the development of some individuals, though it cannot be emphasised strongly enough that their stories are just illustrative and there are many many more who have been touched by engaging with the National Primary Care Collaborative from all disciplines and roles. Personally I remember most those practices and organisations who were encouraged to take part because they were perceived to be underperforming (not that we knew that). They achieved results and grew in confidence simply because someone believed they could do better and they were shown how to in simple ways,

For those who wish to skip to the detail and stick to the macro picture, the boxed summary overleaf should suffice.

It is worth noting once more that the performance of successive waves improved, illustrating the persuasive power of the successes seen to be achieved by their predecessors, and the cumulative transfer of knowledge. The theory translated into practice.

A recent report by the Audit Commission [16] "A Focus on General Practice in England" (July 2003) endorsed advanced access and the Collaborative's approach, recognising the significant impact it had on waiting times, practice culture and teamworking, and the difference it had

> **Results (so far)**
> - 31 million patients in 38 months
> - 72% improvement in access to GPs
> - 80% access improvement in 13 months on wave 4
> - Results repeated in NPDT Centre Collaboratives
> - Fourfold greater reduction of mortality in patients with CHD in Collaborative sites cf rest of England
> - Multiple primary/secondary pathway redesigns and reductions in waits and delays.

made to patients. For that is the ultimate result – the difference this has made to the users of the service, regrettably not frequently enough the measure of work and investment badged as "improvement".

The following sections go into the achievements in greater depth.

Improving access

Advanced access is a logical, practical model with which practices work to improve access. It includes tried and tested ideas for improving the management of patient demand. Not only does advanced access assist practices in reducing waiting times, but it also enables them to offer patients alternative, effective ways to access care, improves teamworking and allows teams to make the best use of their skills.

> **The change principles for the advanced access model**
> - Understand demand and capacity
> - Shape the handling of demand
> - Match capacity of the team to reshaped demand
> - Develop contingency plans
> - Communicate change effectively

The model is derived from ideas on improving access in the USA developed by Dr Mark Murray from the Kaiser Permanente health group. These were adapted and built upon NPDT to become the 'Advanced Access' model. This framework has been further strengthened by the ideas generated by the Collaborative practices and is now being successfully applied in general practice across England.

Measurement for improvement in access

Collaborative practices use the measure of third available appointment to reflect routine availability of clinicians. The measure is based on a simple count of the number of days that a patient would need to wait for a routine appointment with each doctor and nurse in the practice. The next (first) and second next free appointments are not counted as they are more likely to be available due to cancellations. Monthly measurement helps a practice see the impact of their improvements on patient access and is useful in the longer term in proactively managing their system.

Practices also ask a sample of patients about whether they were able to get an appointment on their day of choice. This measure of satisfaction helps the practice understand the impact of their changes on the patients themselves.

Reducing waiting times

The advanced access model has helped practices achieve dramatic, sustainable reductions in patient waiting times.

Many practice teams report frustration and stress due to the waiting times that patients experience. Comments from Sue Farrington, a member of the practice management team at 3rd Wave Lakeside Medical Centre, Bexley PCT are typical of the effect of delays on practice teams:

> 'The feeling throughout the Practice prior to us joining the Collaborative was that of excessive pressure and demand. Everyone appeared to be running to stand still. Doctors and receptionists each felt that they were the only ones coping with tremendous pressure… There was an attitude of "tried that, didn't work, things don't change!"'

Often, having patients waiting means that the work that needs to be done today has to be pushed off into a queue and the situation is self-perpetuating. The advantages of reducing waiting times are clear, for patients and for staff: patients are seen when they need to be seen and staff feel more satisfied in their work. This is reflected in the comments of 1st Wave GP Dr Graham Hillary from Sunnybank Medical Centre in Bradford:

> 'The advantages to the Practice have been that the staff are happier, the majority of patients are happier and the doctors are less stressed. The DNA rates reduced, surgeries run on time and the Practice has started to feel that we are coping and keeping on top of the workload. Unbooked slots have started to appear in the clinical diaries. Additional work is undertaken at peak times, but time removed from the diary when demand is quiet. Visitors to the surgery remark on the tranquil, peaceful and calm atmosphere.' These comments and others

in this chapter reflect the way in which participants themselves spread the work of the collaborative.

To date, the average waiting time to see a GP in Collaborative practices has reduced by 72% (Figure 6.1). There has been wave on wave improvement as learning has accrued during the course of the Collaborative. Wave 4 practices achieved 80% reduction. The Centre Collaboratives are producing similar results.

In many cases, long-standing, lengthy waits have been reduced dramatically (see Figure 6.2)

Individual practices have been able to make significant and sustainable improvements in access to nurses, as shown in Figure 6.3.

Understanding demand and capacity

Practices that have gained most from the advanced access model have worked systematically through all of its components. However, understanding demand and capacity often has a dramatic impact on a practice, and is an excellent place to start improving access.

> 'The task of measuring demand has in itself been a most valuable lesson. Our perception of the level of demand on particular days has not necessarily reflected the actual level of demand on that day.'
>
> Sue Farrington, Lakeside Medical Centre, Bexley PCT.

When 2nd Wave North Brink Medical Practice in Fenland PCT joined the Collaborative, patients were waiting an average of 16 days for a routine appointment. Measuring demand demonstrated two important facts to GP Peter Godbehere and Senior Receptionist Stephanie Large. Firstly, the practice had sufficient appointments each week, but had a backlog that was preventing patients seeing a doctor when they needed to. Secondly, demand on Mondays outstripped capacity unless all appointments were available for patients needing to be seen on the day. They decided not to make any pre-booked appointments on a Monday. This simple change at the start of the week halved the waiting time for a routine appointment within a month. The practice subsequently cleared the remaining backlog and introduced telephone consultations to help handle demand. The practice has now maintained advanced access for over a year.

Understanding the pattern of demand across a week has given practices the information that they need to redesign their systems: follow-ups moved from busy days, especially Mondays; clinics transferred to quieter days and patterns of working altered; all so that patients can be seen when they need to. Different practices implemented different ideas – what suited them.

What was achieved?

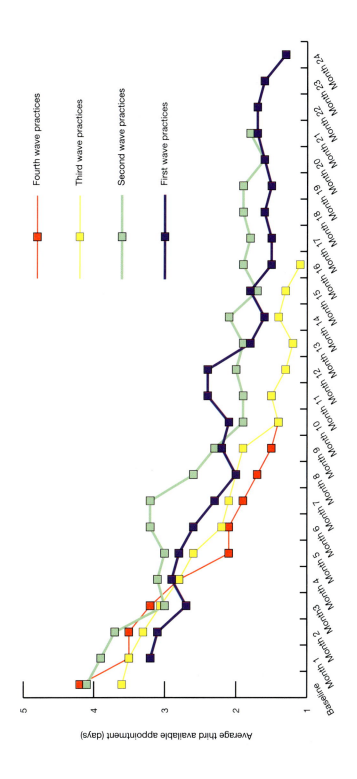

Figure 6.1: GP third available appointment trends
First, second, third and fourth wave practices

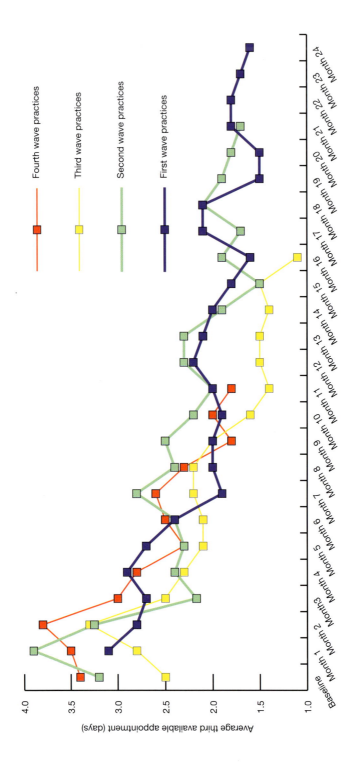

Figure 6.2: Practice nurse third available appointment trends First, second, third and fourth wave practices

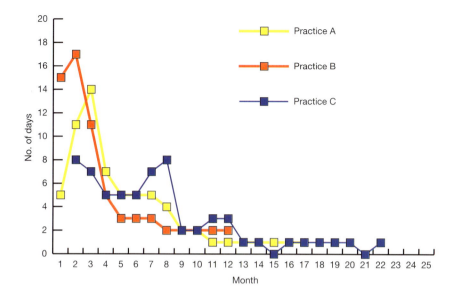

Figure 6.3: Selected collaborative practices
Reduction in nurse third available appointment

Shaping the handling of demand

Exploring different ways to handle demand appropriately means that practices can make the best use of their capacity, and offer patients a choice of ways in which to access care.

'Shaping' in ways such as introducing telephone consultations, telephone management of home visit and same day requests, email for repeat prescription requests and altering the frequency of follow-up appointments creates capacity by reducing the number of face-to-face appointments. Reducing the backlog of long waits means that patients no longer book 'just in case' their condition does not improve and they can't get an appointment, reducing unnecessary consultations and 'Did Not Attends' (DNAs).

'Shaping' the handling of demand often uncovers hidden capacity, which in cases such as Priory Fields Partnership, a 3rd Wave practice in Huntingdonshire, is much needed.

Priory Fields Partnership, Huntingdonshire PCT

When Priory Fields Partnership joined the Collaborative in March 2001, the practice had a 12-day wait for a routine appointment. The first step for GP Andrew Wright and Nurse Sophie Kellen was to measure demand; their analysis showed that the practice was at least 170 appointments short each week. Realising that more could be done with their existing capacity, PDSAs were developed to test out telephone consultations, develop nurse triage and review follow-up practices.

During the course of the Collaborative, the practice ran into a crisis: two part-time GPs left. Despite this, the practice continued improving access, clearing the backlog of appointments and introducing advanced access at the start of October 2001.

The changes introduced by the practice team have freed up hidden capacity: nurse triage has reduced GP face-to-face consultations by 45%, home visits have reduced by 25%, follow-ups have reduced from 47% to 35%. 99% of patients are able to get an appointment on their day of choice, 95% with their GP of choice.

One patient wrote to congratulate the team:

> 'Whenever I phone the surgery or come in, the reception staff are extremely friendly, helpful and most importantly smile! It is now a pleasure to come into the surgery and I would like to congratulate you and your staff for the massive improvements that have taken place'.

Advanced access has also provided the practice with a new approach to recruitment. Based on their new knowledge of demand, the team has developed a precise picture of how much more clinical time is needed to offer patients a high quality service and clinicians a safe, sustainable working environment. A GP from a local practice has been recruited to provide one session of diabetic support and so free up doctor time and a GP has been recruited at eight sessions rather than six to give the team some extra capacity.

Nurse telephone management (triage) of same day demand has become a commonly tested approach to managing demand and ensuring that patients see an appropriate member of the primary health care team. Rather than the traditional concept of triage as a means of defining urgency, the approach is used as a way of managing each patient's needs. Whether by telephone or face-to-face, the interaction is designed to either address the problem there and then or to assess which member of the team the patient should see.

Matching capacity to reshaped demand

As well as looking at simple ways to shift capacity to where it is needed, many practices have looked at developing the capacity within their teams. Optimising how people are working, or developing new skills, can lead to dramatic improvements in access.

Developing skills within the practice team frees up GP and nurse appointments to manage patients in the most appropriate way. As well as shaping demand with telephone and email consultations, 1st Wave Bridge House Surgery in Stratford PCT has introduced a health care assistant, trained reception staff to undertake BP checks, phlebotomy and new patient registrations and introduced nurse-led clinics and new follow-up procedures for HRT, COCP and BP checks. Their GP 3rd available appointment has reduced from 12 days to 1, and the improvement maintained.

Frances Street Surgery in Doncaster PCT has used the advanced access model and their PMS pilot status to develop a nurse-led primary care service. Understanding demand enabled the practice to reduce its waiting times, freeing up capacity to expand nurse work further. The practice has a triage service, minor illness clinics, heart care and hypertension clinics, all of which are nurse-led. Many of the services involve the wider nurse team – District Nurses, Health Visitors and Community Nurses. Nurses handle up to 80% of the practice's demand, and GPs have been able to extend the length of their appointments without working longer hours. The practice has also piloted a patient advice service jointly with the local council. The advice worker can provide personal support to patients on a wide range of non-medical issues. An evaluation based on a group of patients before and after using the service has shown a 30% reduction in GP consultations.

Working with patients to improve access

Understanding what patients think about access has been central to the work of Collaborative practices. Patient satisfaction is measured monthly so that practices are able to track the impact of changes on patients. Many practices have developed other approaches to understand what patients feel about the changes that they have made.

Temple House Surgery in 4th Wave Bath and North East Somerset PCT asked patients a range of questions about their advanced access system. They wanted to find out how easy it was to make an appointment, whether patients got to see the doctor of their choice at a time that they wanted and whether they were aware that they could also see the practice nurses. The results of the questionnaire were very positive about patients' ability to access care: 81% of those questioned thought that the new system was better.

However the study also showed that only around half were aware of nurse advice and telephone consultations. This helped the practice focus their next efforts on improving awareness of these new services.

Second Wave Caldbeck Surgery in Carlisle PCT set up a patient panel as part of their Collaborative work. It has been an invaluable resource in improving their services. Recruitment took place through leaflets in the practice using leaflets and a selection process was designed so that the group would represent a cross-section of their practice population. So far the panel comprises about 60 patients. The practice started out with a questionnaire to ask them about their services. As well as identifying a need for more flexible surgeries and an increased use of telephone consultations, patients flagged up concerns about male and female health issues. As a result the practice has run two focus groups which were well attended by patients. The PCT is keen to spread this approach to patient involvement to all practices.

Lombard Street Surgery in 1st Wave Newark and Sherwood PCT involved their patient participation group in their Collaborative work from the start. The patient group has supported all the numerous changes that have been made to improve access, which include the introduction of nurse and GP triage, telephone consultations, minor ailment slots and self-help information. They have developed information for other patients and collected patient views both formally and informally. The practice has reduced routine waiting times for a GP appointment from 8 days to 0.

When 3rd Wave Yaxley Group Practice in South Peterborough joined the Collaborative, GP Tom Davies decided to invite the Chairman of the Patients' Association to participate in the Learning Workshops. Peter Leaton has attended all three and found them to be immensely useful. 'The Learning Workshops were excellent and my own part in them got better and better. At the last workshop I was approached by a variety of people who realised that I wasn't a healthcare professional and wanted to talk about the work of a patients' association'. Peter was also impressed by the Collaborative approach and the 'genuine desire to spread best practice, to take an idea and slightly change it to suit an individual practice.' Within the practice, the team had regular meetings to discuss any changes that were planned. Peter now also has involvement as a patient representative with the PCT and the local acute hospital and feels that this is crucial for patients in getting a good understanding of the whole system.

Working to meet patients' needs

The advanced access model gives practices a focus for redesigning the ways in which practices are able to meet the different needs of patients. From the first steps of understanding demand to matching capacity to demand within the team and across the week, the changes often provoke positive responses from patients:

> "I am writing to congratulate you on your new very effective service. I telephoned your surgery at approximately 8.15 am for an appointment to see the doctor.
>
> I was offered a **same** day 10.50 AM appointment, which I was unable to accept as I work. I was then offered a 4.20 PM appointment, on the **same** day after being asked what time I could be there. I was informed that my appointment would be with Dr……
>
> On arriving at the surgery at the appointment time, I went to check in and was asked who my appointment was with. Since I had forgotten, the very kind receptionist said Dr……….(who was very welcoming and friendly).
>
> Once again please congratulate all your staff on such a fast effective pleasant service. Well done to you all!"
>
> Patient writing to 3rd Wave Oundle Practice in South Peterborough

Shaping the handling of demand increases patient choice of appropriate ways to access care. Clinicians and administrative staff, especially receptionists, have vital skills in supporting patients to make the best choice about who they need to see and when they need to see them. Many practices have worked with reception teams to develop their skills to help patients choose.

Frome Medical Practice in 1st Wave Mendip PCT use a 'clinical receptionist' to signpost patients to the right member of their expanded team. As well as GPs, patients can be directed to telephone triage, see a member of the nursing or Health Visitor team or a Health Care Assistant (HCA). HCAs undertake ECGs, BP readings, registration medicals, over 75 checks, dressings and primary prevention.

Third Wave Martins Lane Medical Surgery in Wallasey PCT found itself unable to recruit a second GP partner and had to look creatively at how to handle patient demand until they resolved the crisis. As well as making full use of telephone consultations, the practice decided it should take advantage of the nearby walk-in centre. By developing a protocol, receptionists are able to direct patients appropriately to the centre, the nursing team or the GP.

Fourth Wave Project Manager Martin Howard organised a receptionists event for Collaborative practices from Bristol North, South Gloucestershire and North East Somerset PCTs. The event was designed to provide them with a similar environment to a Learning Workshop so that they could share best practice, learn from each other and begin to develop networks. The event proved productive, and popular with the group.

In 2001, NPDT recruited Dr Michael Greco as Head of Patient Involvement. Michael, who had previously worked as Senior Medical Educator within the Royal Australian College of General Practitioners, has vast experience of patient involvement through his work in his native Australia and at the University of Exeter. The Improving Practice Questionnaire (IPQ) and guidance on running Critical Friends' Groups in healthcare settings have proven to be invaluable tools to help clinicians and organisations involve patients directly in improving care. Many Collaborative participants have chosen to use the tool to inform their improvement work and their personal development.

Sustaining improvements in access

Practices that have implemented advanced access have demonstrated that the system is sustainable but that this can only be achieved by proactive, ongoing management. The key is in recognising that advanced access is not an endpoint but a dynamic process.

Having practical contingency plans means that a practice can manage at times when capacity will be reduced, whether expectedly due to holiday or unexpectedly due to sickness or increased demand. Such times can often mean an increased workload for a short time, but it also means that delays do not build up again and the system will return to normal once full capacity returns.

Yarm Medical Practice contingency plans

		F/T	P/T
1	If one GP away for a full week then no change with appointments		
2a	If one GP + Nurse Practitioner away for full week – extra appointments to be put in by remaining GPs over the week:	8	6
b	Drop Administration Session		
c	Nurse triage to continue, but to be the responsibility of the practice nurse covering the treatment room		
3a	If two GPs away for a full week – extra appointments to be put in by remaining GPs over the week:	8	6
b	If needed, nurse practitioner to swap her treatment session for a bookable nurse practitioner session. Other practice nurses asked to cover treatment room as part of their flexible contract		
c	Drop administration session		
d	Cancel practice meeting – then no change with appointments		
4a	If Nurse Practitioner away – then no change with appointments		
b	Nurse triage to continue but to be the responsibility of the practice nurse covering the treatment room		

Popular contingencies include increasing the amount of 'shaping' carried out, particularly the telephone management, and postponing meetings and outside commitments until capacity is restored to the necessary levels.

Sunnybank Medical Centre

Sunnybank Medical Centre is a 1st Wave practice with 9400 patients in Bradford South and West PCT. The practice joined the Collaborative with a third available appointment of 9 days for GPs, and around 160–200 DNAs each month. Their initial measurement of demand showed a shortfall of 20–30% of the total appointments needed. After measuring demand, the practice team have used PDSAs to introduce changes including telephone consultations, group consultations, skill mixing including introducing a Health Care Assistant and Treatment Room nurse and extending the role of the reception team to include phlebotomy. As a result of their understanding of demand, the practice has been able to contract long-term locum cover as part of their contingency plans. The third available appointment is 0 days for GPs and 1 day for nurses at June 2002, 18 months after introducing the changes. DNAs are now typically less than 40 per month, around 1% of appointments.

South Norwood Hill Medical Centre in 1st Wave North Croydon PCT implemented advanced access in July 2000, the first practice on the Collaborative to do so. They have measured demand and capacity since then and, using process control methods, are able to demonstrate that their system remains stable after two years. Their contingency plans include flexing the length of surgeries and converting clinics to routine appointments when GPs are away. The practice has experienced a reduction in DNAs from 12% of appointments to 5%. Demand for out of hours services has also fallen and they have not needed locum cover since they introduced the system.

Freeing up capacity to expand other areas of work

Advanced access has helped many practices free up capacity so that they can develop other work. Moving appropriate work to nurses from doctors, or from nurses to other member of the team, has meant that people have been able to concentrate on priority areas such as elderly care or chronic disease management or pursue other interests.

Porlock Medical Centre

Third Wave GP Ian Kelham works single-handedly at rural Porlock Medical Centre in Somerset Coast PCT. The practice team felt extremely pressurised by the workload when they joined the Collaborative, not knowing when surgeries would finish and how much work to expect in any one day. Major improvements have been achieved by introducing telephone consultations and developing the work undertaken by the nursing team. Ian has been able to pursue his role as Education Lead for the PCT more comfortably and to initiate a local project to develop the role of pharmacists in managing patient demand. Working with the sole local pharmacy, the 'Prescriptions Direct' pilot aims for the Pharmacist to be first point of contact for repeat prescriptions. Eligible patients are signed up by the GP at their medication review and five signed repeat prescriptions are held at the pharmacy. The pharmacist is responsible for verifying repeat prescription requests and identifying any problems experienced by the patient. Early results show increased patient empowerment in managing their condition, more advice being given by the pharmacist, early identification of patients using excessive medication and consistent availability of obscure drugs. Improvements for the practice include a reduction in 'rush' prescriptions, fewer telephone calls to the surgery and less GP consultations.

Equally, moving some of the work traditionally undertaken by nurses to other members of the team such as phlebotomists or health care assistants has enabled nurses to expand their role, particularly in chronic disease management. Princes Park Surgery in 2nd Wave Liverpool PCT has developed the role of Health Care Assistant to support its nurses, and to allow them to expand their own nursing role:

Princes Park Surgery in 2nd wave Liverpool Central West PCT developed a training programme to support the development of health care assistants (HCAs). As well as linking with existing training such as courses in venupuncture and smoking cessation, the practice adapted NVQs for nurses. HCAs now perform a very wide range of duties that includes hypertension monitoring, lifestyle advice, new patient medicals, audiograms, pregnancy and urine testing, ecgs, nebulising and venupuncture. This has freed up nursing capacity for other work which, in turn, has freed up GP time.

Helping with practice development plans

Many practices have found that the advanced access model has provided a practical way for them to implement other developments within the surgery.

As mentioned previously, the advanced access framework has helped practices to match their capacity to demand. Claremont Medical Practice in 1st Wave East Devon PCT wished to develop an integrated nursing team before joining the Collaborative but felt that they had a lack of resources to do so. Using the Collaborative model, the practice measured demand for both doctor and nurse appointments, discovering that they needed to shape the handling of patient demand to make the best use of their capacity. Using PDSAs, they have introduced telephone consultations for GPs and nurses, nurse triage and nurse-led minor illness clinics. As with many other practices, communication with patients through leaflets, posters and in person was vital to the success of the changes. Patient feedback has been excellent and gaps have appeared in surgeries. The practice reports having 'more control of the day's events' and a greater sense of 'working together'. Receptionists are 'delighted'.

Advanced access has also proven invaluable to practices wishing to develop as Personal Medical Services (PMS) pilots. For Eastleigh Surgery in 3rd Wave West Wiltshire, the advanced access framework complemented their PMS plans and gave them the tools that they needed for change. With a list-size of almost 16,000 patients and a minor injuries unit within the practice, the surgery had average waits of 8 days for routine appointments to see a doctor. They felt that demand was 'out of control' and were experiencing high DNAs and considerable stress. Returning from the 1st Learning Workshop, the practice team set about implementing the advanced access framework. They measured demand in detail, including categorising types of appointments requested, and found that around 255 consultations each week were appropriate for nurses rather than GPs. The practice decided to invest in the nursing team, develop protocols for managing common conditions, change follow-up practices, reorganise their appointments system and, to accommodate the new way of working, reorganise their consulting rooms. The practice also developed a new role of Patient Services Co-ordinator, part of whose job is to supervise the appointments system daily. Waiting times for GPs have reduced from 8 days to 1 (with an increase in appointment length), and for nurses from 5 days to 1. The improvement has been sustained since.

Improving care for patients with Coronary Heart Disease

Introduction

The Collaborative's approach to improving care of patients with coronary heart disease (CHD) is based around clinical evidence on the effectiveness of medication and best practice in delivering care.

The approach provides a simple framework which, when implemented systematically, enables practices to maximise health gains for their patients with CHD (see below).

> **Change principles for secondary prevention of CHD**
> - Develop and maintain a valid CHD register
> - Implement agreed protocols for care
> - Use computerised templates for collecting patient information
> - Identify systems for call and recall of patients
> - Develop nurse-led care for CHD patients

Reducing mortality from CHD

PCTs in England have been working to reduce mortality from CHD by implementing the National Service Framework (NSF).

Comparative mortality data has been obtained for PCTs on Waves 1 and 2 of the NPCC, which have been involved for sufficient time to allow a comparison between the twelve months prior to and after joining. During this period, CHD deaths in Waves 1 and 2 fell by over 1000, which is four times greater than the reduction in CHD deaths for PCTs not involved on the Collaborative.

The improvement in Waves 1 and 2 translates to just over 800 extra lives saved compared to the rest of England. Replicating this improvement across the whole of England will result in nearly 6,000 fewer deaths from CHD in a year.

Measuring for improvement in CHD care

Rigorous, regular measurement has been central to the improvement work in Collaborative practices. The discipline of examining and understanding the data at practice level each month enables practices to target their ongoing care effectively.

> 'On CHD we have learned that the monthly audit process is an efficient and relatively easy way of gradually improving care in this chronic disease. By regularly feeding back the figures to clinical staff and discussing ways of improving we have been able to achieve a gradual but highly significant improvement in all the measures.'
>
> Dr David Rivers, Hastings House Surgery, Stratford PCT

Four measures are used, and reported on monthly, which reflect the improvement work on CHD:

- % of CHD patients on aspirin
- % of CHD patient on statins
- % of post-MI patients on beta-blockers
- % of patients with BP < 140/85

The charts in Figure 6.4 overleaf show the shift in each of the measures achieved by 1st Wave practices; these were repeated on other waves.

Achieving multi-disciplinary ownership of patient care

In many Collaborative practices, a small, multidisciplinary team has been responsible for this area of work. Using PDSAs to introduce rapid change, the teams have worked systematically to improve the register, check prescribing and medication compliance and recall patients. The process has led to a clear sense of multidisciplinary ownership of the care of these patients, and has led not only to significant improvements in the quality of registers but also in the ongoing care of patients shows how Dr Mangat's practice in 3rd Wave Ealing PCT worked with PDSAs to improve their care in a planned, systematic way.

The Collaborative team of Practice Manager, Practice Nurse and GP has used PDSAs to improve the quality of the register and the care that they provide. The PDSAs achieved:

- A complete CHD register, validated against patient notes
- The identification of patients not already included on the register
- The introduction of tracer cards to notes to identify CHD patients to doctors and nurses
- The identification of patients that have not had a review in the last 6 months for follow-up
- The introduction of telephone review of non-attenders based on a nurse-developed template

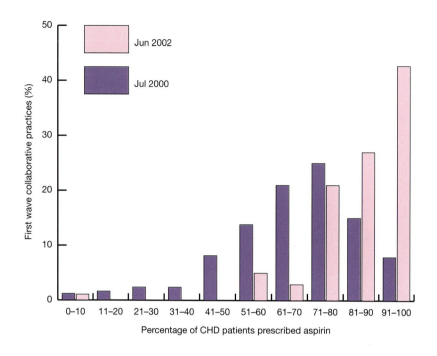
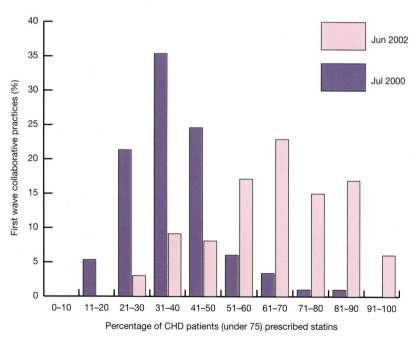

Figure 6.4

What was achieved?

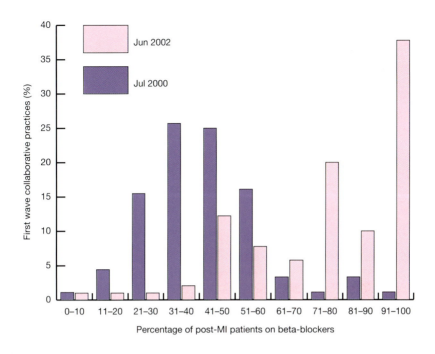

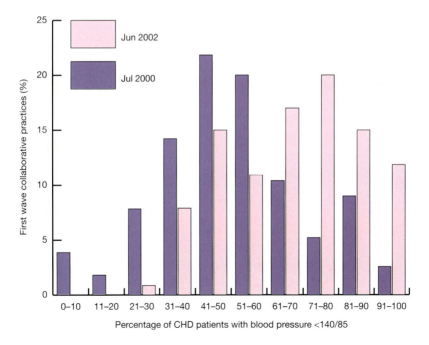

Figure 6.4 (continued)

- Newly developed patient literature on statins and beta-blockers in English and Punjabi, and a survey of patient views on it and changes in their knowledge resulting from it
- The identification of CHD patients that smoke, offering support to quit
- The identification of a need for exercise classes suitable for Asian women and working with an Asian women's centre to arrange classes
- The involvement of a local Community Pharmacist to support patients with medication compliance providing an individual plan to help the patient remember doses and understand the action of each drug and to support patients with queries or concerns
- Collaborative *m*easures of: aspirin 96%, beta blockers 100%, statins 77%, blood pressure 70% at June 2002.

Developing effective Nurse-led care

The Collaborative has demonstrated the effectiveness of nurses in managing patients with chronic disease such as CHD. The majority of Collaborative practices have chosen to transfer much of the work to practice nurses, often in tailor-made CHD clinics.

In some cases, practices have identified a need to free up nurse time for the work and have introduced or expanded phlebotomist or health care assistant roles, tying in with the work that they have done on improving access.

Many PCTs have adopted and supported the approach across all practices. In Easington PCT, a 1st Wave site, the practice nurses from the collaborative practices took the initiative to drive the CHD work forward:

> From the outset, Easington PCT supported a nurse-led approach to improving care for patients with established CHD. Nurses from the Collaborative practices were given authority to lead the work. Continuous liaison with other clinicians involved in delivering care was a prerequisite. Led by Carol Hardy, who is a specialist nurse in CHD, the nurse team:
> - Developed a PCT-wide strategy for structured care for patients with established CHD
> - Developed a partnership approach to provide comprehensive care across all settings
> - Produced valid CHD registers
> - Developed templates for gathering information and protocols for ensuring consistently managed care

- Implemented a system of audit and strategy to meet training needs
- Liaised with GPs to ensure their agreement to developments
- Liaised routinely with Coronary Rehabilitation Nurses at local acute trusts
- Collected monthly data on CHD based on the Collaborative measures
- Measured patient satisfaction with the changes.

PCT support for the Collaborative approach

Improving care for CHD patients has been a priority for all PCTs, and many have developed initiatives to support practice work in this area including funding additional nursing time, providing facilitators to help improve data quality and linking with secondary care to improve acute services.

Third Wave South Stoke PCT joined the Collaborative at the start of their journey to improve CHD care:

> Prior to joining the Collaborative, South Stoke PCT had provided additional funding to increase nurse time for CHD and diabetes management, and carried out a baseline survey of practice-based CHD management. The PCT had yet to identify a lead manager for CHD or develop standardised templates or protocols. First steps were to nominate the NPCC Project Manager, Sandra Chadwick, as lead manager. Sandra quickly designed a CHD template that was made available to all practices. The Collaborative practices used PDSAs to develop and maintain registers and plan call/recall systems. Nurse-led CHD clinics were established, the PCT piloted the introduction of a Health Care Assistant to free up nursing time for CHD management and funded Heartsave training for the nurses themselves. A further 20 practices have since adopted the approach. Working with Sandra, the Collaborative practices have produced a protocol for secondary prevention of CHD for use across the PCT. Sandra has also worked with the local Acute Trust and Heart Failure Liaison nurse to establish a weekly nurse-led Heart Failure Clinic within the PCT. She represents the PCT on the CHD Local Implementation Team and Cardiac Network group, and works with the Commissioning Manager on the Local Modernisation Review for CHD. Three nurses have been trained as assessors to support the ongoing work of the HCAs. Work has now moved on to heart failure management.

Project Manager Heather Marsh from 2nd Wave Doncaster PCT involved all 11 practices in the PCT in the Collaborative work on CHD and was particularly keen to disseminate the improvement method as well as the Collaborative CHD framework to practice teams. Working with the British Heart Foundation trainer, Fiona Mackie, Heather taught on the managing change module of the HeartSave course for nurses, which was run district-wide. Her sessions included the use of measurement and run charts to understand demand and capacity for clinics, using PDSAs to introduce rapid change and project planning for CHD clinics.

First Wave Stratford PCT has developed a new care pathway for patients during their first year post-MI. The work, developed with the Collaborative practices and the local acute hospital, includes an assessment tool for reviews at 0, 3 and 6 months and the use of the Hospital Anxiety and Depression Scale (HADS) for post-MI patients.

Innovating in CHD care

Many practices have used the improvement model to develop innovative approaches to improving care for patients with established CHD or to extend their work to wider CHD care.

GP Spencer Nicholson's team from 1st Wave Nelson Fold Practice in Salford PCT needed to find a way to manage the workload generated by CHD reviews and to maximise the number of patients attending. They decided to call patients for an annual Heart Check around their birthday, and send Happy Birthday invitation letters to patients to remind them of the importance of attending. Early results were positive – 118 of 139 patients invited have attended.

Dr Mangat's surgery in Southall and West Ealing had a significant problem with non-attendance for CHD reviews. They have introduced nurse telephone management of non-attenders, using a practice-agreed protocol for interviewing patients about their health, medication compliance and lifestyle.

Temple House Surgery in Bath and North East Somerset PCT (see 'The Improvement Model' section) have expanded their work on CHD to include understanding demand and subsequently expanding capacity for CHD clinics, introducing health checks for all men aged 50–60 years of age and improving their stroke/TIA register.

Practice Manager Debra Wheatley and GP Mark Sanderson from Spinney Surgery in 3rd Wave Huntingdonshire PCT also decided to target male patients at risk from CHD. They held a Men's Health Evening, providing cholesterol, blood pressure and glucose testing stations and issuing

'MOT Certificates' at the end of the session. Advice was available on a range of issues including healthy eating, exercise and relationships and healthy food and 'freebies' such as tape measures were provided. One patient was identified as having significantly raised cholesterol levels. He usually attended the surgery infrequently and his problem was unlikely to have been picked up otherwise.

Capacity and demand management – improving access to routine secondary care

Background

When patients enter secondary care, they already have a relationship with primary care, and will return to primary care, once their visit or stay is completed. Primary care professionals have a unique perspective on, and involvement in, the patient journey and it is for this reason that capacity and demand management is part of the NPCC.

> **Advanced access between primary and secondary care – understanding demand**
> Understanding the number of referrals, pattern of variation across the year, causes of variation
>
> **Shaping the handling of demand**
> Standardising referral processes through the use of protocols and guidelines, peer review of referrals. Developing alternative ways of handling demand: email advice and consultation, patient self-care, telephone triage or consultation, triage systems and use of GPwSIs (GPs with a higher skill in a particular area e.g. dermatology)
>
> **Matching capacity and demand**
> Understanding capacity and making the best use of it e.g. scheduling; 'pulling patients through'; optimising capacity e.g. looking at waiting list shapes, booked admissions; reducing the number of queues; reviewing staff and equipment availability to put where most needed; looking at skill mix e.g. GPwSIs, specialist nurses and PAMs (physiotherapy, occupational therapy, etc.)
>
> **Establish robust contingency plans**
> Ongoing measurement of demand, 'horizon scanning' for changes in demand or capacity, plans for holiday and sickness, flexible clinic times, increasing shaping to cater for increased demand

> **Ensure effective communication**
> Finding effective ways to communicate change with staff and patients continuously

Principles for capacity and demand management

The basic framework of advanced access can be applied at any point in the patient journey between primary and secondary care. .

Huntingdonshire PCT has implemented advanced access in dermatology outpatients. The service, which once had waiting times of 36 weeks, now has a 4-week wait that has been sustained since October 2001. Redesigning the pathway in partnership with the local acute trust, a PCT-employed GP with a Specialist Interest (GPwSI) was introduced to manage patients not requiring a Consultant opinion. Referral protocols were agreed with GPs, demand measured based on weekly referrals and the backlog cleared with extra sessions. The administrative officer running the booking system is responsible for identifying any problems with demand and capacity, and the flexible capacity of the GPwSI is regularly called up to maintain the waiting time.

Supporting capacity and demand management work

NPDT has trained NPCC Project Managers in the tools and techniques that have proven effective in capacity and demand management work, providing their Primary Care Trusts with a unique resource to progress this area of work. Project Managers have played a crucial part in moving the work forward:

> 'From the acute point of view, the best thing that has happened was having a (NPCC) access manager in the PCT and a shared agenda between primary and secondary care'.
>
> Clare Allen, Access Manager, Gloucestershire Hospitals NHS Trust

The tools and techniques used, although simple, are important in beginning to identify areas for improvement and in facilitating change. Mapping of the processes involved in the patient journey, or 'walking' the patient journey itself, can highlight unnecessary or rate-limiting steps or identify hold-ups.

Learning Workshops for Collaborative participants and bespoke 'Capacity and Demand Management' days for wider audiences of primary and secondary care professionals, have exposed sites to leading edge examples of improvement at the primary/secondary care interface. To begin with, exemplar sites, often from other modernisation programmes, were drawn from across the country to share their work but increasingly the stories have come from work developed by Collaborative sites themselves.

It was recommended that Collaborative sites establish a steering group to oversee the strategic plan for capacity and demand management. At the same time, Collaborative teams were asked to start work by looking at a single problem specialty. In many cases it was a specialty with long waits where GPs from Collaborative practices felt they might play a direct role in influencing change, where there were already links with clinicians in secondary care that were keen to improve services or where improvement initiatives were already underway.

Third Wave Wallasey PCT used the route map to get started in capacity and demand management:

Wallasey PCG (now PCT) started by setting up a high level steering group straight after the 1st Learning Workshop, with representatives from primary and secondary care. With 17% of all patients on inpatient and day case lists waiting for ophthalmology procedures, the Collaborative practices and PCG identified ophthalmology as a priority at the 1st Learning Workshop. The practices set about monitoring the number of GOS.18 forms received from opticians to understand demand and then linked into an existing acute-trust pilot of direct referral to an optometrist.

The Collaborative Project Manager, Jenna Odley, then linked up with the Booked Admissions Project Manager at the acute trust to identify other current work. Jenna and a GP from one of the Collaborative practices attended a Urology away day, mapping the patient journey and identifying potential improvements. The process led to agreement to an intermediate service to filter out less complex cases. A GP training post was proposed based in a local community hospital, working alongside the consultants. Other plans for redesign include nurse triage of referrals and standardising pre-referral assessment tests to prevent duplication and speed up the patient's journey.

All of this work was progressed within a year of the 1st Workshop. Jenna further developed links with the acute trust through presentations to the Modernisation Team and Directorate Manager's meeting. Orthopaedics was the next specialty targeted by the steering group, and a working group was set up. Their initial work has highlighted the potential for reducing the existing waiting list through the validation of long waiters.

Stockport PCT, a 2nd Wave site, established an 'Access Task Force' to act as a steering group for capacity and demand management and whole system access issues. The PCT and local acute Trust have agreed a long-term strategy to move approximately 30% of secondary care outpatient activity into primary care over the next 10 years. As a health economy, Stockport has brought together a number of complimentary initiatives – the Primary Care Collaborative, Action on Orthopaedics and the Booked Admissions Programme – to support the modernisation agenda. During 2002–3 four new services, involving extended role practitioners, will be launched. These are musculo-skeletal triage using a GPwSI and extended scope physiotherapists; primary care-based dermatology staffed by GPwSIs and specialist nurses; an extended primary care mental health service and a direct-referral cataract service. The work under the NPCC and other initiatives has supported a whole system approach to service redesign, facilitating buy-in from clinicians in both sectors, and ensuring that the planning of services was already complete when funding became available.

Using simple techniques to bring about change

Collaborative sites have drawn on the expertise of their Project Managers in current techniques to bring about improvement.

The Collaborative team in 3rd Wave Bexley PCT started work on knee problems within Orthopaedics and held a process mapping day that was well attended by primary and secondary care clinicians and managers. Delays, bottlenecks or steps that did not appear to add value were identified in four areas: referral to first outpatient appointment, referral for physiotherapy and MRI scans, appointment for pre-admission clinic and surgery. A further meeting highlighted three areas for focus: quality of referral, pre-assessment and physiotherapy. A sub-group was set up to look at physiotherapy triage, scoring systems for hips and knees, review shared and self-management for two conditions (osteo-arthritis and anterior knee pain), audit of outpatient referrals to identify how many were avoidable, review of pre-assessment and direct booking, understand capacity in secondary care.

To date, there has been agreement to an extended scope practitioner (ESP) in physiotherapy and GPwSI, use of the Oxford scoring system, review of the physiotherapy pathway (currently long waits and high DNAs) and to develop guidelines for physiotherapy referral. Funding has been secured from the ESP.

Fourth Wave South Liverpool PCT set up a steering group straight after the 1st Learning Workshop in and held a process mapping day the following month, looking at a relatively small but important problem of delays in glucose tolerance tests (GTTs). An initial analysis of waiting times suggested patients would wait 6–8 weeks for their results. Working with the acute trust, the NPCC Project Manager found that the real wait was at least 12 weeks and that 130 patients were waiting, of which 40% were from South Liverpool. The Consultant agreed that the work could be carried out at a local Primary Care Treatment Centre, and protocols were drawn up for the new pathway for GTTs. Within 4 months, the backlog of tests had been cleared through an initiative by the acute trust. The Treatment Centre now undertake all GTTs for South Liverpool residents, and will expand this service for patients further afield shortly. There is no wait for GTT results for South Liverpool PCT patients. This initiative was undertaken with no additional costs, just reshaping of capacity at the treatment centre.

Fourth Wave Watford and Three Rivers PCT has used the improvement model to test out the idea that telephone access to a Cardiologist would reduce avoidable referrals. Two GPs and a Cardiologist from the acute trust agreed to review 79 referral letters. The results showed that the majority of referrals could have been managed through telephone advice with investigations subsequently organised. As a result, the Cardiologist agreed to pilot a telephone advice service for Collaborative practices. A Consultant will be available on a dedicated telephone number each day for two hours to offer advice. If it is agreed that a patient requires further investigation, they will be referred directly, omitting the usual outpatient appointment. Measures have been defined including the number of patients that would normally have been referred to outpatients, the number that avoided an outpatient appointment and patients' views of the service.

Project Manager Aly Valli from 1st Wave South West Oxfordshire PCT used the improvement method and developed a Clinical Improvement Worksheet to take forward the redesign work in dermatology. The Worksheet was based on work from the Institute for Healthcare Improvement based in Boston, USA and was designed to guide people through the process of making decisions about change. Using the approach with primary and secondary care clinicians and managers led to an agreed approach to testing change in service delivery. Two pilots were selected: introducing GPwSIs and tele-medicine. Two community-based, GPwSI-run clinics were introduced and two further clinics planned. The formal introduction of tele-medicine has been delayed by technical problems but GPs are sending digital images informally. The waiting time for appointments at either of the community clinics is 4 weeks.

Shaping the handling of demand in primary care

Many of the initiatives to reduce delays between primary and secondary care, like the examples included from the NPCC, look at new and appropriate ways of handling demand in primary care. GPwSIs, specialist nurses and PAMs are delivering care in partnership with secondary care colleagues, often in primary care or community facilities, improving access for patients.

Eastleigh Surgery, a Wave 3 practice in West Wiltshire PCT with over 15,000 patients, looked at how they might improve care for patients with mental health problems within the practice. As a result, they reduced referrals to secondary care by 83%. Their approach involves developing a programme of care for each patient and providing appropriate support from a team that includes a CPN, a Counsellor trained in mental health disorders and two GPs with a special interest in mental health. The practice has developed a mental health register, self-help packs, and uses a care pathway and rating scales. Any patients referred to secondary care are fully worked up, and secondary care has secure access to practice server and patient records. As well as the reduction in referrals, GP consultations for anxiety and depression have reduced by 23%. The mental health team has shared its learning through the NPCC and many practices have taken aspects of the approach to develop their own services.

Redesigning patient pathways to improve services

Some of the improvements achieved in Collaborative sites have been based on relatively small inexpensive changes to the way services are delivered. Liverpool South PCT's change to the glucose tolerance testing service is a good example of a small change that has a large impact on patients.

In 4th Wave Bristol North PCT, one GP felt that palpitations testing should be carried out in the local community. Clevedon is some distance from the acute hospital, and patients have to make two visits to complete the test. A small group of clinicians and managers, including the Collaborative Project Manager, Martin Howard, has planned the service move and from October 2002 the Cardiac Technician will be carrying out the test at a local cottage hospital.

In South Stoke PCT, the pathway for dermatology has also been redesigned. The Collaborative practices, Chief Executive and Consultant Dermatologist worked together, agreeing that a possible 70% of referrals could be managed in primary care, and developing referral criteria and protocols. A GPwSI was recruited. Referrals in the first quarter comprised patients from the existing secondary care waiting list and direct referrals from GPs. Including existing referrals, waiting times during this period were an average of 3.5 weeks. Those patients referred directly from GPs have waited an average of 1 week. This compares with previous average waiting times for a Consultant of 26 weeks. 5% of patients have been referred on to the Consultant.

Other initiatives have been more extensive. Coventry PCT, a third wave site, also decided to focus on dermatology at the 1st Learning Workshop. Working initially with Collaborative practices, waiting lists were validated and protocols developed to ensure all referrals are recorded in the same way. Plans were developed to reduce the surgical backlog by diverting cases to a local GP who is a secondary care provider. Other achievements include creating routes for patients to be treated within primary care such as piloting "store and forward" teledermatology with specialist nurses and increasing capacity for cryotherapy within primary care.

Huntingdonshire PCT has piloted a telephone self-referral service for physiotherapy with two Collaborative practices, covering approximately 24,000 patients. Referrals can be made directly by the patient or through the GP, and patients are given a telephone number for the service, which is available for 4 hours each day. The physiotherapist is able to screen, diagnose and provide appropriate management over the telephone. Patients receive a written copy of the advice in the post the next day, and a copy of the assessment is sent to the GP. Any patient that needs a face-to-face appointment is seen within ten working days.

Only 30% needed a face-to-face appointment with the remaining 70% being given advice for self-management of their condition. There was a saving in physiotherapy time of over 380 hours in the first 6 months. DNAs are less than 1% compared with 15% before the pilot. Patients and staff suggest increased satisfaction through having instant access to a physiotherapist, reduced waiting times, lower costs, fewer hospital visits and reduced community physiotherapy visits.

Building relationships between primary and secondary care

One of the greatest investments for primary care in this area of work has been in developing relationships with colleagues in secondary care. Many Collaborative Project Managers have found that progress has been slower than the work on primary care access, yet it has been the efforts to identify key people in local acute trusts that have paid dividends.

3rd Wave Southampton PCT

In 3rd Wave Southampton PCT, early Collaborative work focussed on management of the Coronary Artery Bypass Graft (CABG) waiting list. The Consultant prioritises patients for surgery based on a scoring system. In addition, the PCT and acute trust hold monthly meetings to actively manage the waiting list: many of the patients have coexisting conditions and their eligibility for surgery can alter. This initiative has reduced waiting times from 15 months to eight, and more importantly, has been invaluable in developing an understanding of the 'difference between managing rather than just monitoring the waiting list'.

Ronnie Burlinson, Project Manager in 1st Wave Easington PCT, invited the Clinical Directors of Orthopaedics from the two local acute trusts to the Capacity and Demand Management Day. At this event they agreed to focus on reducing delays for patients with knee problems by ensuring that referrals go through the knee service, in each case involving an Extended Scope Physiotherapist, rather than to a named Consultant. Any patient needed to see a Consultant after assessment would be guaranteed direct access.

Within 12 months, no patient was waiting more than 13 weeks for an out patient appointment within Orthopaedics, a significant improvement. At City Hospitals Sunderland NHS Trust, similar results were obtained. Before the initiative, waiting times for a Consultant appointment were 22 months

2nd Wave Gloucester and South Tewkesbury PCT

In 2nd Wave Gloucester and South Tewkesbury PCT, NPCC Project Manager Lisa Proctor linked up with Clare Allen, the Access Manager at Cheltenham Hospitals NHS Trust. Working with GPs from the Collaborative practices, secondary care clinicians and managers, several initiatives have evolved. A direct access hernia service with nurse-led pre-admission clinics and fast-track referral has been introduced. A new pathway involving a GPwSI and nurse-led pre-admission clinics has been introduced for patients with suspected adult tonsillitis. In orthopaedics, a new hips and knees pathway involving physiotherapy triage is in place. This includes an electronic booking system that allows GPs direct access to physiotherapy appointments and a physiotherapy telephone triage service. The triage service cost only the price of a new telephone line to establish.

The reason for illustrating the stories alongside the bold statistical results is to give a feel for the sort of ideas and experience gained by a participant at a workshop. Many of the participants want on to learn more about improvement science, and developed themselves as well as their organisations.

Developing people and organisations

This section highlights some individual stories: how people, and the organisations that they work in, have developed as a result of their involvement in the Collaborative. The people mentioned here are just a few of the many who have made personal journeys as a result of the Collaborative, but their stories illustrate the growing development of the capacity and capability for improvement methods within organisations that was the prime objective.

Sharing stories locally, nationally and internationally

Presenting at workshops has become a regular event for some practice teams. Dr Peter Godbehere and Stephanie Large from the North Brink Surgery in Fenland PCT have told their story in practices and at local and national events including the NHS Confederation. Peter has presented at the European Forum for Quality in Health Care in Edinburgh and at the International Summit on Idealised Design in Clinical Office Practice (IDCOP) in Chicago, USA, and is now representing NPDT in developing work with Saskatchewan, Canada.

Hazel Hunt, Practice Manager from 1st Wave Claremont Medical Practice in East Devon PCT presented at the IDCOP Summit in Atlanta, telling the practice's story of developing an integrated nursing team as part of advanced access.

Dr Ian Rutter, GP and Chief Executive of 1st Wave North Bradford PCT, has provided ongoing support to the NPCC, particularly around the topic of capacity and demand management. Ian has presented at the Institute for Health Improvement's International Forum on Quality Improvement in Health Care in Miami. North Bradford PCT won the Prime Minister's award for outstanding achievement in 2003, as well as best PCT. Ian generously attributes their success to implementing improvement knowledge throughout the activities of the PCT, particularly its commissioning role.

Joan Booth – Practice Nurse to PCT Director
Joan Booth had been working as a practice nurse for 24 years when North Sheffield PCG was accepted on the 1st Wave of the Collaborative in June 2000. Joan was frustrated by the kind of problems with access that many practices experience: 'It felt like demand was insatiable, patients had to wait up to two weeks to see me or be fitted in between other patients. I had a DNA rate of up to 20% and spent my lunch times catching up on administrative work and nursing duties. I felt like I was fire fighting but never had time to find out what was causing the fire'. Encouraged by colleagues, Joan was successful in her application for the post of NPCC Project Manager.

After twelve months in post, and due to the successes of the Collaborative in North Sheffield, Joan was approached by the then Trent Regional Office. They were keen to start to spread the Collaborative work more widely. The PCT negotiated to keep Joan for two days a week to continue her work locally. Joan's regional work, endorsed by NPDT, included designing events mirroring the national workshops for people to learn about improvement, and working with PCT Chief Executives to develop plans for improving access. The learning in Trent informed the model of working for NPDT Centres nationally and when expressions of interest were sought for PCTs to become NPDT Centres, it seemed natural that North Sheffield PCT would apply. Successful in its bid, Joan was appointed as Lead Manager of the East Midlands NPDT Centre at the start of 2002, and in 2003 was promoted to be a Director of Modernisation in Oldham PCT

Dr John Bibby – incorporating the improvement method in local education
Participants in the 1st Wave of the Collaborative will know John Bibby as a GP from one of North Bradford's core practices. John has also regularly shared North Bradford's 'SOAP' story: how the Shipley Ophthalmic Assessment Programme reduced waiting times in ophthalmology. Fourth Wave practices will also know John as Clinical Chair of their Wave. NPDT was keen for John to take this role with the final Wave of the Collaborative as a result of the changes he introduced as PCT Education Lead in North Bradford. Learning about the improvement model inspired John to build the approach into practice and PCT education programmes. At his practice, Windhill Medical Centre in Shipley, both practice and personal development plans include the PDSA approach to testing changes. PCT education is also firmly based around the improvement model to bring about action learning: protected learning time and monthly practice-based education include the development of PDSAs. NSF, Clinical Governance and professional groups also use and share the results of PDSAs.

John as an affiliate of NPDT, has been involved nationally in helping design some of the new IT systems for the NHS.

Michelle Coleman – from Receptionist to Patient Services Manager
Michelle was a Receptionist at 3rd Wave Eastleigh Surgery in West Wiltshire when the practice joined the Collaborative in March 2001. In implementing advanced access as a PMS pilot, Michelle moved into a new role, Patient Services Manager. Michelle likens the 16,000 patient practice to the Starship Enterprise, with her role being to keep the ship on course. Michelle has presented her work on the day-to-day management of advanced access to audiences from across the country, describing how she

maintains the system through measurement and monitoring, and communication with the whole practice team about their part in sustaining the improvements.

Dr Mark Hunt – Director of Clinical Leadership Development, NPDT
Mark Hunt is a GP and was Chair of Mendip PCG, a 1st Wave Collaborative site. Mark attended the Learning Workshops with GP colleague Nick Whitehead, who was responsible for implementing advanced access across the four site, 30,000 patient practice. Mark became a keen advocate of the Collaborative approach and his leadership qualities made him a clear candidate for the role of Clinical Chair for the 3rd Wave of the Collaborative. Mark now heads the West Country NPDT Centre, hosted by Mendip PCT, and has recently joined NPDT as Director of Clinical Leadership Development. Mark will be responsible for establishing opportunities for personal development for primary care clinicians involved in NPDT programmes who wish to develop their leadership skills. Through support networks and development programmes, he is taking forward the aim of NPDT to create a mass of individuals in primary care who have skills in leadership and quality improvement.

Gill Bell – from PA to Modernisation Manager, Huddersfield PCT
Gill was in on NPDT from the start, having been appointed as my PA. For a number of years before that she had been secretary to a consultant neurologist. Gill, alongside Michelle Smith, another early recruit to the admin team, rapidly learnt how to run a workshop for 300 people – collaborative style!

She developed a keen interest in the work, and the methods underpinning the programme. As part of her personal development she took part in the project manager training that took place. This led to a secondment to a PCT to assist in their modernisation programme, which through her own efforts led to a substantive management post. Within 2 years a total and successful change in career. Michelle Smith also took the skills she had developed into events management, being part of the control centre team for the highly successful Commonwealth Games in Manchester in 2002.

▬ The story continues

In this chapter we have seen a snapshot of what participants have achieved for their patients – and how they have developed. The Collaborative continues, the people sustain the work in their own organisations, the measures haven't slipped. Improvement is a human effort driven by the desire to do better for those we serve. The methodology is the route map.

7

Sic evenit ratio ut componitur – again

The past chapters have illustrated how the concepts of systematically transferring knowledge, stimulating an environment for change, and developing a strategic framework and infrastructure for spread have been the cornerstones of the large system change we have sought to achieve. Within those broad headings are a number of practical steps to take, not least paying close attention to social and psychological aspects of change.

Large system change is underpinned by work on the diffusion of innovation and obtaining a critical mass. This has been achieved by the NPDT by phasing the Collaborative's work:

- *Phase 1*: 4 national waves covering 20% of Primary Care Trusts, and 20% of the practices within them.
- *Phase 2a*: 11 NPDT Centres created in sites of the national waves, themselves trained in the relevant methodologies and running regional Collaboratives; collectively, NPDT and its Centres have engaged with every Primary Care Trust in the country.
- *Phase 2b*: The 11 Centres operating a second wave of Collaboratives in their patches on the same topics, enhancing their expertise.
- *Phase 3*: At this point the infrastructure is in place to spread improvement in a particular topic (or topics) to practices in every Primary Care Trust in England within nine months of commencement. Phase 3 of the collaborative, beginning at the time of writing, exemplifies how this can be done. The topics are improvement in the management of diabetes and chronic airways diseases, and this time patients are active members of the improvement teams.

Skills are constantly being transferred, and leaders identified and developed to create sustainability and to increase the capacity and capability of primary care organisations. The NPDT Centres, following Phase 3, will be fit, within their designated geographies, to respond to local imperatives as well as to assist subsequent national agendas. The continued national linkage is, however, vital in maximising the further spread of new innovations from one part of the country to another. The maturation of the lead managers and their teams within the Centres has been impressive. They and their teams have experienced a customised development process, tailored to their perceived needs as well as those perceived by the national team. The network that has been created between them has consolidated them as a group, but also created an environment for what might be termed competitive co-operation.

There is a friendly rivalry about how well they each operate their Collaboratives, and the workshops and the innovations they have created. Some of these innovations have been adopted by the national team centrally. The two-way process, the freedom to travel and gain new thoughts, seeing what goes on elsewhere, are reminiscent of the consequences of trade and travel across the Roman Empire.

The one less than perfect element of the infrastructure, and where in retrospect we might have erred slightly, is in the creation of facilitators in each of the Primary Care Trusts, themselves relating to the NPDT Centre. The error has not been in the concept but rather in the execution. The difficulty has been that some Primary Care Trusts have sought to use facilitators for non-core purposes; in other PCTs they may not have had appropriately senior line management; and in a very small number of cases the individuals were not up to the task. Others have been quite outstanding: where the post has been operated as envisaged the results have been impressive, particularly in engaging more practices in the process. The learning is that we should have been more prescriptive about recruitment, salary and line management in exchange for the funding provided.

The generic learning for large system change remains constant: seek out, recruit and train effective local influencers of change.

When is a system a large system?

How long is a piece of string? The answer to these two questions is identical – it depends. People in my own world might say that primary care is only part of the large system, and that it is the whole larger system that needs attention. This is to ignore the fact that primary care deals with 80% of all activity in the NHS. People sometimes talk of 'whole systems' in reverential, politically correct and even emotional terms. This is chocolate box villages, English summer days, cricket on the green and Miss Marple cycling along the road – not to mention apple pie. In one sense they are right: a holistic view is important. But holistic views do not of themselves force change. Indeed they probably make it look impossible.

Our experience is that a major part of creating the environment for change is understanding the *particular* setting and culture in which you are working, making people feel familiar enough and hopeful (and then confident) enough to start looking over the boundary walls that separate sub-systems. Above all we must be focussed and determined about manageable objectives, and unswervingly objective and self-critical about what is being achieved.

In other words, by starting in a circumscribed way, and gaining success, people gain the volition to move beyond their own environment. The holistic picture is built up in pieces, and is easier to realise in our view.

> "The programme has taken joint working to another level that puts patients at the heart of the process."
>
> a GP in Croydon

> "The programme has helped my understanding of system design within a hospital and assisted in my executive role on the PCT with regard to commissioning."
>
> a GP in Ecclesfield

> "The programme has made me think more globally, look at problems in a different way".
>
> a hospital Consultant

These comments are taken from post-workshop evaluation sheets; they started to look over the boundary walls; their driver; the care.

So what did the Romans do for us?

The Romans, in creating their Empire, gave us precedents which 2000 years later hold strong in large system change. But readers may have asked themselves, as they patiently tolerated my metaphor, whether it is polite or relevant to recall that the Empire collapsed.

Proper historians will relate a whole sequence of events and factors, but the bottom line was that they started to lose the values upon which their principles and policies had been based. They became more inward-looking, self-satisfied and less curious. This gradually allowed their hungrier, relatively deprived, less complacent and highly motivated enemies to erode and eventually defeat them. They, the incomers, did not value knowledge in their culture. They stifled or neglected communication, stopping the flow of people and ideas. The skills died out: 1200 years of the Dark Ages.

The principles underpinning our work are those of continuous rapid improvement, achieved by people in the system. The value system governing it is about caring passionately for the patient. We have seen in other parts of the health sector, where the principles have been diluted by an impulse to manage improvement 'in the style of' existing conventional hierarchical systems, that the energy and vitality of even enlightened methodologies get ossified by bureaucracy.

The majority of people working on improving services clearly hold to the values of care equally passionately. Yet, paradoxically, as improvement as a concept has attracted larger investment and more prestige, we can observe projects started and continued for the benefit of the *project* in the face of sparse results. On occasions personal ambition exceeds ambition for the service. As the Romans would put it, "sic evenit ratio ut componitur" – translated, every system delivers exactly the results it is designed to give.

The epilogue

The example given in the booklet has been the Primary Care Collaborative, whose topics (access to primary care, the management of a disease within primary care, and access to secondary care) meant that the whole patient journey was covered in one programme. However, a holistic view recognises that interaction with other agencies and organisations in respect of social care etc is of equivalent importance. For this reason we run two other collaboratives, the Healthy Communities Collaborative and Falls Collaborative, which straddle these elements of the system.

Figure E1 sums up the strategic approach adopted by NPDT.

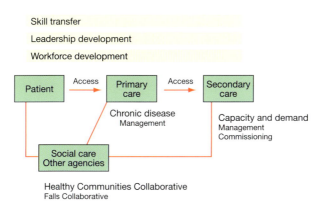

Figure E1

The Healthy Communities Collaborative is worth a slight diversion. In a sense it brings us full circle to the question of what is a large system, since although it fits into the scheme in the Figure above and is part of that system – each site seeks to address a local system change across agencies and across disciplines

── The Healthy Communities Collaborative and other systems

The Healthy Communities Collaborative is unique in the sense that 65% of participants are elderly residents in the deprived areas we are working with. The remaining participants come from a variety of organisations, voluntary, local government, health, social care and contain an equal variety of disciplines. The hypothesis constructed for the Healthy Communities Collaborative was whether assisting teams within a community make improvements in a particular topic would gain sufficient social capital for them to tackle other topics. In this process they would begin to create positive changes in their environment as a whole. As the participants worked on a topic, in parallel they would also be seeking to implement the change principles we had identified that seemed to underpin successful conventional community development projects. This hypothesis I call Community Action (see Figure E2).

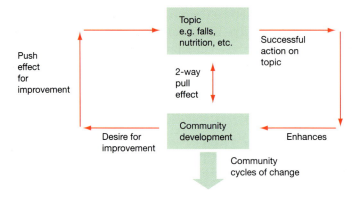

Figure E2: Theoretical model for community action

In this multi-agency, multi-disciplinary environment our learning was that paying detailed attention to getting teams functional prior to attending a collaborative workshop was a crucial factor. This was expertly achieved by Linda Henry, the director of this programme.

The story is almost worth a book in itself. Suffice to say that this group of older people have transformed themselves from a more dependent mode to being vocal, proactive influencers of change in their communities. Collectively, they have demonstrated a 32% reduction in falls in older people, as measured by calls to warden services (a remote on-call service manned to assist people in difficulties) in their areas within seven months. The sites are now progressing to work on nutrition, involving younger people in the same localities. However, the networks they have created have spanned into all sorts of smaller projects, e.g. how to reduce crime in handling rogue callers. Witnessing what they have achieved and hearing them present is a humbling and moving experience. If they can achieve change of that dimension in that timescale, we professionals have no excuse. The Healthy Communities Collaborative recently won the award for addressing inequalities at the NHS equivalent of the Oscars.

The experience in the Healthy Communities Collaborative and the interaction with other organisations reinforced our view that the principles and practice outlined in this booklet were transferable to other sectors. NPDT, at the behest of the Department of Education and Skills, has just commenced working on an analogous programme with schools, led by Liz Twelves. The topic is under-performing boys, which itself has ramifications in the health sector since underperforming pupils have a greater chance of poor employment with the health consequences of that poverty (when is a system a large system?!). The rules are the same, clearly taking into account the different culture and environment. The first learning workshop felt like the first one of the Primary Care Collaborative in terms of its energy and atmosphere. And interaction with these other sectors allows us to see things that, modified, would work elsewhere – sharing knowledge and implementing improvement across "divides".

The replicability of the method is reinforced by each discussion and every project we undertake. I say this in no sense to claim that the principles we have derived are the only ones applicable to achieve large system change, nor that it may be appropriate in every circumstance. Clearly there are likely to be a set of different principles around a performance management operation to achieve large system change. My point is simply that the method we have used is transferable to other areas, other environments, other countries. The learning continues, the curiosity remains and the family of improvement grows.

Bibliography

1. Berwick, D.M. (1989) Continuous improvement as an ideal in healthcare. *New Eng J Med* 320, 53–56.
2. Langley, G.J. *et al.* (1996) *The Improvement Guide*, Jossey-Bass, USA.
3. Pasmore, W., *et al.* (1982) "Socio technical systems", *Hum Rel*, 35, 1176–1204.
4. Hardy, C. (1985) *Understanding Organisations*. Penguin.
5. Deming, W.E. (1986) *Out of the Crisis*. Cambridge, MA.
6. Juran, S.M. (1983) *Managerial Breakthrough*. McGraw Hill.
7. Shewhart, W.A. (1980) *Economic Control of Quality of Manufactured Product*. Milwaukee, Minn.: American Society for Quality Control (originally published 1931).
8. Ishikawa, K. (1985) *What is Total Quality Control – The Japanese Way*. Prentice Hall.
9. Donabedian, A. (1980) *Exploration in Quality Assessment and Monitoring*. Health Administration Press, University of Michigan.
10. Batalden, P. & Nolan, T. (1994) Knowledge for Leading the Continual Improvement of Healthcare. Manual of Health Service Administration, Aspen.
11. Weick, K.E. (1995) *Sensemaking in Organisations*, Sage, California.
12. Rogers, E.M. (1998) *The Diffusion of Innovation* (4th edn). New York: Free Press.
13. Gladwell, M. (2000) *The Tipping Point; How Little Things Can Make a Big Difference*, Little Brown.
14. Plsek, P. paul.plsek@directedcreativity.com
15. Cooperrider, D. & Srivasta, S. (1987) "Appreciative inquiry in organizational life", *Research in Organisational Change and Development*, Vol. 1, 129–169.
16. Audit Commission (2003) *A Focus on General Practice in England*.